Women in Transition
(I am a Wanderer)

By

Margaret Brisco

PublishAmerica
Baltimore

First printing

ISBN: 1-4137-2845-6
PUBLISHED BY PUBLISHAMERICA, LLLP
www.publishamerica.com
Baltimore

Printed in the United States of America

This book is dedicated to my children Annamaria and Ralph, to the memory of my grandparents, and to Gery, my beloved ghost.

Acknowledgements

I would like to acknowledge the following people without whom this book would not be possible:

To my children, Annamaria and Ralph—without their loving support and help, I would not have been able to publish this book.

A special thank you to my daughter Annamaria for her active role in producing this book by correcting, editing, and advising me.

The Chameleon Women, Thelma, Vera and Elaine, writers, poets and story tellers.

"The Group:" Dr. Milton Shoshkes, a physician, teacher, and scholar; Thelma Johnson, "the goddess," friend and fellow writer; Tony, the cello player and Ed, the sexy gentleman.

Lynn Dodd who helped type and correct my manuscript.

Tunnelvision and my friends Virginia Angelovich, Rosa Soy and Diane Devlin.

To Virginia Angelovich and Lynn Vergano, thanks for your support and advice.

And to all my other friends and supporters whose names are too numerous to mention, but to whom I am eternally grateful.

Table of Contents

Prologue: The Group

"I would like to read for you," she said. "If you like it, you tell me that you do. If you don't like it, you tell me anyway. And I will leave. 'Con la coda fra le gambe, come un piccolo cane randaggio, (with my tail between my legs, like a little stray dog),' as my old grandmother used to say."

"Is Italian your primary language?" He listened to her strange accent and could not place it. "So few Europeans come to our shores these days."

"Yes and no," she answered. "Many languages, many dialects and some long forgotten. Some coming back in spurts, in spite of not wanting. I am a wanderer. I am also an old woman."

"Where is your wandering taking you in those days?"

"Nowhere in particular. Perhaps here. Perhaps into writing. The last hurrah."

They are walking up the stairs to the second floor of the Goddess's home. Up above, on the second floor, the generation of multiples read their stories.

"I am going to read a story about life and a story about death."

"An American death?"

"Perhaps. Perhaps not. You decide."

"Do you want to be published?"

"I do," she said, "I do."

They are sitting around the round table in the Goddess's library-sitting room. The wanderer is watching them: each of them has a name. Not the conventional name that you put on a driver's license, or on your passport. It is the name that they carry in their silences, in their songs, in their laughter and perhaps in their sorrows.

The cello player.

The sexy gentleman (with a capital G).

The old soldier.

The professor.

And the Goddess.

The wanderer watches and thinks: "If I leave now, I will not be missed. I will take my Mercedes E 320, my dog and some books. A CD or two, Mozart and perhaps Chopin. (I am not that knowledgeable about music.) Drive to California. I will live on the beach. Live in my Mercedes and sleep in it. King will bark and no one will come close."

But she knows that this is only a fantasy. There is no place in this world where she can park her Mercedes and sleep in it. Or walk on the beach and bathe in the ocean. And let King bark.

So she sits in the Goddess's library, which is filled with ancient figures from ancient times, with pieces of ancient rituals and ancient icons. They are looking at the group, wondering why they are intruding. Is the Goddess their peer? Is the Goddess a thousand years old?

The cello player.

The sexy Gentleman. (with a capital G)

The old soldier.

The professor.

The Goddess.

The wanderer watches and thinks, "Isn't this perfect?"

Part One:
Women in Transition

To Have and To Hold

RUTH

It is for some time that I have lived here in this place. I suppose it is not a bad place to live, but I really don't care about the people here. They are not my family.

I plan to write a letter to my daughter. I have a daughter who must be grown by now, but I really don't know. She is not a child. She is not old either. Anyway, I must write to her. I must remind her of the times when we went swimming together, took riding lessons, and played tennis together. I remember that she was so special; so strong, athletic and fearless.

What has happened? Where is she now? Did I invent all of this? I remember Jack, my husband, well. He comes to see me often. He has a smiley face, blue eyes and a long nose. His hair is gray now, but I remember when it was ash blond. He was such a charmer. We would go to the shore in the summer and swim, sun and walk on the boardwalk.

Did I have a daughter? I must write her a letter. She must think that I don't care about her anymore. But that is not true. Did she abandon me? I must find out why.

I believe that I started to forget things after Ellena left, but I'm not all that positive. I would forget to shut off the light or to turn off the motor of the car. But where did she go? Her father does not tell me. He still has a smiling face with wrinkles around his eyes from laughing, but he won't tell me anything about my daughter. I am starting to think that perhaps we never had a daughter...

I don't remember exactly when I stopped teaching. I know that

11

one day I walked into my classroom to find another person teaching my class. I became very angry. I insisted she should leave. She had no right to take my place. I knew that I was shouting. Then I saw my husband and he took me away and brought me home. I was very upset with him—how could he take their side? He was the one that had always stood by me. I calmed down eventually, but I never went back to teaching—just stayed at home, thinking and trying to remember.

I have to write a letter to my daughter.

Dear Daughter: Are you trying to forget me? Your father comes to see me and I ask about you. He gives me vague answers and then I forget his answers. I also ask him about himself, the house and the neighbors. I want to go home. I want to go home and talk to you. I want to ask you why you have abandoned me. I am frightened and upset at the thought that you are not here. I want to go home. Your father tells me, "There is no home any more, sweetheart. I live in another place and have sold our house." "You sold our house?" I scream and cry, and then he leaves and I am once again alone with strange people. I ask, "Where is my daughter?" But nobody answers. Nobody cares.

Did I have a daughter? Maybe not. But I am writing to you just the same in case you get this letter and decide to visit with me.

Dear Ellena, it is not bad here. People talk to me and I answer back, but then I get tired and walk away. I walk outside to look for you, but someone always brings me back in. I try to explain that I want my daughter who has left but will come back for me.

I have to wait for her so that she will see me and not get lost in this place. "Have a cup of tea," they tell me ignoring my wish.

"I don't want your tea!" I scream and then go back to my room. My husband comes to see me. Sometimes there is a woman with him. It is not my daughter. She has a fixed smile on her face and small, deep-set foxy eyes. I ask my husband, "Who is she?"

"A friend," he says and she smiles a sly smile, looks at me with her foxy eyes and says, "Hello."

I wonder why she is here with him and I don't like it.

'To have and to hold' comes to mind. I don't know why, but I say out loud, "To have and to hold." But then my mind wanders and I forget that the woman is there with him. Instead I think of my home and of all the things I have left and I ask, "How is the house?"

"There is no house, sweetie," he says again.

I freak out and shout, "I want to go home." He walks away and I continue to scream until he is gone and the woman is gone with him.

I am alone again with strangers. I walk down the hallway and the hall seems interminable—long and winding with eyes from doorways watching me while I walk.

The woman had a fixed smile with small shrewd eyes. Who is she? I don't like her.

Once again I am writing a letter to my daughter:

> *Dear Ellena, please come. I am ill and live in a house that is not our home. This is an institution. It is not bad here. People are nice and patient. This morning when I refused to get out of my bed, they got me out, washed my hands and face, and helped me to get dressed. I don't look pretty anymore. You have my dark eyes and pale skin, and you are beautiful. You are like a bird with an elegant neck and smooth feathers, and I am lumpy and formless with a face that has lost all its expression. Is my soul leaving me? Where are you? What are you doing these days? I am waiting for you—just waiting and waiting.*

My husband comes alone. There is no woman with him.

"You are not eating, " he tells me. "You are losing weight."

"Are you waiting for me to die?" I ask and he frowns and answers quickly, "No, of course not."

The answer is too quick, and I don't trust him. His eyes are getting smaller and they begin to look like the eyes of the woman he sometimes brings with him. He avoids looking at me. Is it perhaps because I am no longer pretty? I am thin and my clothes hang on me—shapeless like empty sacks. I hate to eat.

"You have to eat," he tells me.

I promise that I will start eating. I don't want to die. I want to go home.

I wake up after a long sleep. I am lying in bed and the bed's sideboards are up and I have an IV drip in my arm. It is a hospital bed. I am in a hospital. My husband is standing next to me with the woman with the sly eyes. She is not smiling but staring into my face as if expecting something. There is no daughter. I have no daughter. I suspect she has never received my letter. I look around and all of a sudden all is clear to me.

I say to Jack, "You are leaving me and she is with you now. You sold my house and I have no daughter. You are abandoning me so that you may marry her."

"Why are you leaving me?" I whisper.

He looks at me and I see tears in his eyes and he softly says, "You have abandoned us long ago."

I remember the church, the music and the flowers. I remember his sunny, smiley face. "To have and to hold," I whisper softly and look around me once more and gradually, I feel darkness embracing me.

ELLENA

I went to see my mom today at a nursing home where my dad put her after her mind deteriorated so much that he was unable to cope. Poor Dad! A big part of his years have been spent caring for mother. It is almost inconceivable that she has deteriorated so. When I went to see her she did not recognize me. I found her sitting in her rocking chair, the same chair that she used to rock me when I was a little child. It seems such a long time ago...rocking back and forth, back and forth.

"Hi, Mom," I said, "How are you?" I touched her cheek gently and left my hand resting on her face as she used to do to me when I needed her love, care and strength. She looked at me vaguely and did not respond.

"It's me, Mom. Ellena. Don't you recognize me, Mom?" I stroked her face again and bent down to kiss her. She turned her head away and continued to rock, staring blankly at the wall.

"You are the lady that lives next door and always wants to know what is going on in my house. I have never liked you. Go away. I don't like nosey women."

"I am Ellena, Mom." I said again.

She replied, "Who is Ellena? I don't know any Ellena."

I touched her cheek again without trying to kiss her. I left a box of cookies on her nightstand and left.

There are no Ellenas and no moms anymore in her world. My father has another woman now who spends a great deal of time in his home. Her name is Marie. She is younger than he, smiles pleasantly when I visit and tries to be nice. But I don't like her. I think of her as an intruder. I am a grown woman now and should not feel this way, but I do.

I went to see my father after the visit in the nursing home. He had previously sold our home and now lives in a townhouse in one of those communities that caters to the better-off middle class. We were seated across from each other in his modern kitchen having an espresso. I told him of my meeting with Mother. He nodded his head and said nothing.

"Dad, I am leaving for good. I don't want to be here anymore. When I find a new job I will write to you."

"I am sorry, Ellena," he tells me avoiding my eyes. "Is it because of Marie? I just cannot be alone anymore. Marie is nice, caring and we go places together. She has no children of her own. She probably would like to have you around."

"I'm sorry too Dad, but it really is better if I leave. I really have no reason to stay. When I find a job I will write to you. Take care of yourself," and as an afterthought I add, "and of Mother."

I felt like a coward and despised myself. We hug each other briefly. "So long, Dad."

"So long, Ellena," my father says.

JACK

It is finally over, our years of togetherness and then the slow journey into the darkness. The journey has come to an end and Ruth's funeral was the ultimate solution to all. Do I feel relief, a sense of freedom or perhaps a sense of betrayal? Did I betray a wife who abandoned us—me, her husband, and her only daughter? Did she relentlessly fall into an abyss in which there was no place for the two of us? I have lived with her progressive loss of memory, her loss of feelings but with occasional flashes of consciousness—short realizations of who she was but reverting back to hostility, rage, rejection and confusion.

Ellena came to the funeral. She was too late to be present at her mother's death. Following a heavy snowfall, it was a December day with brutally cold weather accompanied by merciless winds. The remnants of the heavy snowfall had transformed the top layer of snow into ice that was smooth as glass. People were sliding dangerously. Women with hats were wrapped up in furs and everyone was braving the cold wind. In addition to all of us, there were heaps of frozen earth, reddish and clay-like, around the deep and unfriendly grave in spite of the wreath, flowers and a friendly pastor delivering a compassionate sermon.

Ruth had wanted to be buried next to her parents. We slowly lowered her casket into the family grave. We threw flowers on top of it and said our last goodbyes. Ellena stood next to me. We held hands like a pair of lost children clinging to each other with the cold crushing our chests as if our hearts were being deprived of the last drops of blood.

Marie was at the gravesite but did not stand next to us. I did not offer my hand to her. This was Ellena's pain and mine—the pain of lost years when Ruth was there but was not, and we were not able to be there for her since she did not know us anymore.

I am returning to my flat alone. Ellena is going to stay with me for a few days. We will talk, perhaps have a few meals together, an espresso or a cup of herbal tea in the afternoon. Then she will leave to go back to her job, promising to be in touch.

Marie is around, patient and waiting, but for a while, I just wish to be alone with my pain and my memories.

The Boredom of Living
(A Love Story)

She belonged to an old "mitteleuropean" family with some aristocratic ties on her mother's side. She used to say this occasionally, in conversation with her friends at lunch.

When she was growing up, they had a butler, a maid and the cook. At that time, she was not allowed into the kitchen, since the cook was a neurotic and a hysteric, and the kitchen was totally his domain. No intruders accepted.

The family moved to the States before the onset of the Second World War. Their move was also the end of the luxurious lifestyle they were all used to since her father abandoned a very lucrative business with corporate connections in many different countries. It was nevertheless a very wise move. Wise and lucky. Were they Jewish? Was the father Jewish? Possible and probable, but Ernestine did not know and did not ask.

She was moderately religious, attending a church on Sundays and at times, weddings, christenings, and funerals.

Many funerals.

She was not a youngster.

She was close to being eighty years old and a widow for more than ten years.

Ernestine professed to have loved her husband very much, and was sincere about it. Love is difficult to define. As physical as it may appear, it still remains, for the most, an abstraction. So she loved her husband. She had been pampered by him, he who was much older than she. Ernestine was like a child to be spoiled.

****

The husband may have been impressed by her breeding, her natural tendency to be elegant, but also by her ways to be coquettish, flirtatious, insouciant. That was her goal in life.

Her marriage had been arranged by her parents who, in their opinion, had concluded he was the right choice for their daughter.

She accepted that, and it came very natural to her. It suited her well. Her feelings were not deep, and she did not engage in any intellectual exercises.

When her husband died, Ernestine was very sad. So now she was an older woman living alone: though none knew her exact age, since she hid it with great expertise from all her friends and acquaintances, and pretended to be much younger than her real age. Her walk was as bouncy as a ballerina, her body slim, and she made regular visits to the hairdresser, the manicurist, the pedicurist, and to exercise classes. Thus, her body remained "young."

Since she had spent her young days flirting, having fun, throwing languid glances at young, handsome men from good families, her concept of herself was of someone who has had a wonderful youth. An unforgettable youth that she still remembered vividly, even at her age.

Living on the East Coast of American suburbia, she spent lots of time having lunches with other middle-aged ladies. Being secretive about herself, Ernestine had no real friends among women. She did have a good number of men friends who interestingly were attracted to her: the gay ones, the heterosexual ones, some of them of certain age, handsome and not so handsome. She would attract them, as a female insect with pheromones would attract partners during the mating season. Ernestine definitely had pheromones. Hers was a need for a man to be near her, not as a lover or a mate, but someone who would cater to her and serve her as a medieval troubadour had served his chosen lady, or Dante has served his Beatrice.

She was no Beatrice. She was close to being eighty years old.

And so time went on.

****

Ernestine met Leo at a time when she decided to take lessons in ballroom dancing.

In her town, ballroom dancing was becoming quite popular. There were Fred Astaire Studios and others less well-known, but equally successful studios with an older crowd of couples and singles. Especially with single women. It was a good place to exercise, have fun and possibly meet new people.

Leo was a dancing instructor in one of those places. Thin and elegant in a tuxedo and a trim mustache, dark eyes and hair that was sleeked off with some sort of cream or gel since not one hair was ever out of place.

He had embraced many women in the course of his career as a dancing instructor, mostly as a routine, smiling into their eyes without passion. He never got an erection when dancing with them cheek-to-cheek, or performing a passionate Argentine tango. Some of the women were reasonably attractive and possibly were taken by him. That was good for his business.

When Ernestine joined the dancing studio, Leo instructed her as he did instruct all others. But for Ernestine, the more she danced with him, the more she wanted to continue dancing.

She thought: "He will never see my breasts, but if I am close to him I can feel his chest close to mine."

She was proud of her breasts: they were solid with pink nipples and dark areolae, making them, well, desirable.

Ernestine would snuggle close to him, and in the beginning he did not respond. But slowly, Leo started to keep her close to his body whenever the dancing permitted. She was thinking, while looking into his eyes admiringly and smiling one of her famous seductive smiles, "He has such a perfect body, such a marvelous chest. His face, his hair, his eyes."

They continued to dance like that for quite some time. Then Leo started to favor her. At times when a special step had to be demonstrated, he would choose her and at the parties given by the school he would dance with her more than with any other pupils. "Why do you favor me Leo?" she would ask with an innocent smile and a twinkle in her eyes, her red-blond hair in place. "Because you are different," he would say. And she was different. The pheromones.

The first time Leo had invited her for a late lunch, they drove together, there, to a little restaurant on the Jersey shore, all well and proper. It was an intimate lunch with smiles and an occasional laughter, and with no great depth to the conversation, because perhaps, they were both frivolous people.

Leo, what are you doing with an eighty year old, you who do not get an erection while dancing body to body with so many women?

****

Ernestine was not looking for an affair; it was sufficient for her to play these juvenile teenage games. She thought of herself as being "proper." Her mom would have approved. Her wish was that she would be looked upon for her aristocratic behavior, her coiffure being properly done, her clothes "well put together" with a pocketbook and shoes to match. Her jewelry sparse, only a diamond ring in the forth finger of her right well-manicured, right hand.

So vain for an old lady. An old lady that stayed "young," because of not knowing what suffering or having passions meant.

Leo, by now, was telephoning as often as three times a day. She would pick up the phone and there he was calling her name in a whispering sort of a way.

"What are you doing?" he would ask. "Are you watching television? Did you have your lunch? Did you have a glass of wine?"

"I do not drink," Ernestine would answer, "but I have a chocolate after lunch."

"What kind of chocolate do you like?"

"Perugina kisses," she would say, and he would add laughingly, "I wish I were a Perugina."

It was all very innocent or it appeared to be so.

Then the calls became steamier with sexual overtones and

innuendos. "Are you in your bed?" he would ask, calling in the evening. "Do you have silk sheets?" Ernestine would answer laughingly, flattered that a young, handsome man might be interested in her bedding. It never occurred to her that he might have had his own arousal while imagining her between her silken sheets.

She had to admit that she herself was aroused by this conversation. Afterwards, she would lie in her bed dreaming about things that she knew she should not be doing. There was no way that she would admit him into her dreams or into her home.

"May I come in?" he would ask after one of their lunches together, which they always had out of her town.

"No, you may not," she would answer, and in her mind she would worry what people would say. "I live alone and it is not proper."

On a similar occasion, when he took her home, she suddenly asked, "What would you do? Would you throw me on my bed?"

"No," was the answer, "I would be very gentle and loving."

She offered her hand to say goodbye and he kissed the palm of her hand. Ernestine withdrew her hand quickly and walked alone into her home. She was slightly frightened. Living in the same town all her life, Ernestine was worried that rumors might start about her, she who was always so impeccably well-behaved.

"I have to stop this," she said getting herself into her bed. "But I can certainly dream. That is not forbidden," she thought as she drifted off to sleep.

****

He started this flirt with her, as he did start so many, because this was his business, part of his routine. Out of professional obligation, Leo danced with many women, smiling, looking into their eyes and holding them close. It was all innocent, frivolous, and to a point, proper. Something that was expected from a dancing teacher. Many women came there for the pleasure of socializing and to meet other people. Some also for the pleasure of music and the elegance of ballroom dancing.

He loved to dance, but did not like to teach dancing. It was repetitious and monotonous. Boring. Mostly older people, some really elderly. Leo danced with them voluptuously, teaching them various steps. Most of them would learn well. Some came in couples, which was good. It was nice that he did not have to smile so much.

She asked him once, "Why do you like me?"

"Because you are different," he remembered answering and that was true. So different from who he was and who he had been.

He was an orphan with no mother and with no father. He was raised in an orphanage by kind nuns.

Leo always told people that his mother died in childbirth and that his father had abandoned him. But the truth was different. He had imagined this young girl, his mother, (just imagined her since he did not know her at all) who became pregnant and thus disgraced her family and herself. Perhaps she was run out of her little town or village in the northern Alps, where he was born, and had wound up somewhere on the streets of a big city. Possibly, some kind man may have married her, and when the occasion occurred, reminded her for the rest of her life of her sinful past, making her life a living hell. Leo had no way of knowing.

He was good-looking in a certain effeminate way. When he grew up and was on his own, after many trial and errors, he became a dancer.

****

Leo has a partner now, a dancing partner. She is also his wife, but Leo is not in love with her. He does not think that she is in love with him, but they dance beautifully together and it is worth it for them to be together. Leo thinks, "We both enjoy each other's dancing and dancing with each other. The rest is routine."

Ernestine is an older woman. A lady. As most of my pupils are. Ballroom dancing is not something the very young wish to pursue. She snuggled close to me, looked into my eyes and had a very particular smile. Innocently sexy, I should say, inviting and yet proper as it would be expected from a woman of her stature. Thin, very well dressed reddish blond hair and the smile. This smile.

Under different circumstances, I could have been the son she never had. She, an upper class child brought up with a governess in a household with a cook, and a butler, and I, fatherless and motherless with the wonderful body of a dancer in a perfect tuxedo and with the face of a Rudolph Valentino.

I am dancing with this lady, holding her close to my body and she is smiling at me with a twinkle in her eye, and she is full of sex appeal.

The great democracy.

The world of today.

We became friends. I became obsessed with her. We would talk on the phone. We would have coffee or lunch together and lots of laughter. Then I bought myself a two-seater, a red Ferrari convertible (used of course) and I called Ernestine. I invited her for a ride in my new sport convertible. Just the two of us.

"Where are we going?" she asked on the telephone after taking my call.

"Nowhere special. It is summer. We may go to the shore area and walk on the boardwalk. Or have an early dinner in one of the restaurants there."

She did not answer promptly, and I understood that she might be worried about her friends seeing me with her alone.

"Please come," I said in my throaty voice "I want you with me."

How did she take this? I was waiting anxiously. Then she said, "I will meet you in the parking lot of the Starbucks café." And she hangs up.

****

"I must be dreaming this up," Ernestine thought to herself. "I should really stop this 'back and forth' with this man. It is unseemly. What am I doing?"

Then she thought: "He is so handsome. He has such wonderful body, such a chest. And he dances like a man-angel, light-footed and strong at the same time. Dark eyes, beautiful face."

"Let me go just this time. Not anymore after this."

25

Ernestine could not resist; she was young at heart. She will never become old. She will never have blue hair. Her hair was blond with reddish highlights and she wore dark glasses to camouflage the bags that were forming under her eyes. Her clothes were impeccable. Her purse and shoes always matched.

They met in the parking lot at Starbucks, he in his red convertible, she with an elegant Hermes scarf on her well-coiffed reddish hair.

There was no one she would know in the parking lot, which made her feel good.

Why am I so concerned? she thought. *I am not doing anything wrong. It is only a ride to the seaside.* She still felt slightly uneasy.

He helped her into the convertible and they drove away.

"Let's not go to the shore area," she said, "let's go somewhere else."

So they took the New York Throughway to the mall, where they had dinner in the little dainty restaurant in the mall off the Throughway.

They laughed and talked and held hands.

"You have beautiful hands," he said, and it was true. Her fingers were long and delicate, well manicured and with a diamond ring on the third finger of her right hand. Her only piece of jewelry.

They strolled through the mall, like two adolescents holding hands, window-shopping, looking into different stores. Away from home, not worrying about nosy neighbors, Ernestine felt like a young girl again, walking with a boy of her liking and having great fun.

Returning back to her home with a late sun in their faces, her scarf fluttering in the wind, they felt exhilarated and happy as if the rest of the world did not exist.

But reality was there at her front door when they reached it.

"May I come in?" he asked, looking into her eyes as if wanting to mesmerize her.

There was a moment of hesitation, a moment long in waiting. A great moment when all could have changed. The time had stopped for them as if it was waiting. Waiting for Ernestine to make a decision. For better? For worse? It may be exciting, sinful, passionate. Perhaps also painful.

And then Ernestine said: "No, you may not. Thank you for a marvelous afternoon. I will always remember. I will see you in the ballroom."

She entered her home, and he stood silent, watching. Then he left for his car.

Driving, he felt deflated and ordinary. An ordinary fellow, driving home in the evening after a day's work. He kept thinking about his unusual attraction for this older woman. It had promised to be adventurous, but it ended and the end was almost banal.

Are we banal people? Leo thought. *Let me get to my home and to the wife. We dance well together but there are no magic moments, no fast heart beat. We do have a home, a profession, and the commodities of the modern life style.* Not so bad, he thought again getting to the door of his modest home.

****

Ernestine entered her home and sat on the chair for a while, removing her scarf and blouse. Then she took a hot shower and put on her silk nightgown. She got into her bed and felt her body being warm and wanting. Touching her breasts, she found them to be hard and swollen. She took off her nightgown, and lay nude in her bed. She caressed her bare breasts and then slid her hands down her thighs.

"I am going to have a dream now and imagine Leo next to me in my bed," she said to herself, "There is no harm in dreaming."

Kim

(from the diary of a woman doctor)

I think of her often. I wonder how long it took for her to die and whether it was a painful death. We met briefly. She became my patient, but not by choice. Admitted through the emergency room while I was on call that week, I first saw her in her hospital bed.

Her abdomen was huge, distended by an enormous tumor that had been diagnosed as a teratoma in the emergency room by a sonogram. It was pressing on her intestine and obstructing her urinary tract. She had been unable to urinate, and the pain and discomfort had brought her to this hospital bed.

Her body was emaciated, her legs and arms were painfully thin. Her elongated neck held a Modigliani-like head with transparent beige-colored skin and her two almond-shaped eyes were staring into the world with anger and hostility. She was severely anemic and spoke in harsh whispers, tiring easily.

Her name was Kim. Kim was HIV positive and the teratoma, released under the influence of the disease, had grown into something grotesque and ugly—like some slimy creature from the netherworld.

Those were the early days when we all irrationally feared the disease and we would clothe ourselves with eye shields and double gloves, rubber boots and rubber aprons, not realizing that the only way to transmit the disease was by blood, such as with a needle stick or by a cut from a scalpel. Our rubber boots and rubber aprons were no protection at all.

When I saw Kim in her hospital bed, I brought my own hostility with me, resenting the fact that circumstances forced me to perform the surgery on her and expose myself to the danger of becoming infected. She seemed to know how I felt. She saw the self-protective attitude I had and saw beneath my cool exterior, which was trying to mask my discomfort, fed by the fear of a disease that we did not know how to treat or even how to approach.

Kim possessed the loneliness of the incurably ill, and a cruelly ironic freedom of someone who did not have to adhere to niceties. She looked past me with contempt, the whites of her eyes tinged yellow from a lack of hemoglobin. She had difficulty focusing.

I gave her a consent form to sign. She took a long time to read it, partly because of her weakness, partly in a deliberate attempt to let me wait. I myself made a feeble attempt to explain the text: "And if the tumor is malignant, we should also remove the uterus and the other ovary. You wouldn't want to have anymore children under those circumstances."

"Don't tell me what I want and what I wish," was her reply. "I am a grown woman and make my own decisions."

I turned and left the room. I left her with papers to sign, wishing silently that she would not sign them. Then I would not have to perform the surgery on her. But she did sign them because there was no other choice. The tumor had to be removed in order for her to continue living for as much time as she had left.

I returned to her and ordered what was needed to prepare her for surgery. Kim received blood transfusions and continued the indwelling catheter that had been inserted in the emergency room on admission, to relieve her urinary retention. Her blood values were now being returned to normal. I also prescribed a high protein diet with vitamins and iron supplements.

By the next time I saw her, she had improved greatly. Her skin had acquired a healthy glow, her eyes were less hostile, and she started to look more like a woman living in the present than like a model for a Modigliani painting.

It was then that I saw the photo on her night table stand and cautiously asked, "Who is this?"

"That is my little girl," was the answer. A child with tresses and bows in her hair and a big radiant smile was looking up at me from the picture.

So Kim had a daughter. She was a mother who, not so many years ago, possibly in this very same hospital, was going through the pains of childbirth. How different was her pain now. Did she acquire the disease from an unfaithful lover, or by sharing a dirty needle in a moment of desperate loneliness? I never asked. But Kim became a person to me, someone with a child and a life of her own. Someone to treat and to help to heal.

A colleague and I did the surgery on her a few days later. The tumor was large, as we had expected, with soft necrotic areas and a greenish discoloration. But it was not malignant and we did not have to remove her uterus and the other ovary. After removing the tumor, we rinsed the pelvic cavity, counted needles, instruments and sponges, and began closing the surgical wound.

We were very relaxed at this point, talking casually to each other and to the nurses. It was then that, recklessly and carelessly, I stuck myself with a suturing needle.

I tore the double gloves off my hand, and turning away from the operative field with a sterile sponge, I dried the blood off my punctured finger. The circulating nurse immediately emptied half a bottle of betadine on my hand. I was given another double pair of sterile gloves and we finished the surgery in silence. I left the operating room and stayed at home for twenty-four hours, not talking to anybody.

Kim never knew what happened. When I saw her again, she was recuperating nicely after her surgery. Her healing had progressed well. Her blood levels had remained stable and she was ready to be discharged. She was relaxed now, more mellow. Hope was with her again.

The day she was ready to leave, she looked at me. Anger and hostility no longer colored her face. Smiling, she said softly, "Thank you Doctor."

"You are welcome, Kim," I said as softly as she and nothing more was said. We were friends then, if only for a moment.

She was referred to the rehabilitation unit and I never saw her

31

again.

That was a long time ago. For Kim probably a whole lifetime. And for me, times of silent worry, uncertainty and waiting. During those long months I thought of Kim often, of how unkind I had been to her and of how my own fear of the unknown had turned me hostile, remote, and lacking compassion.

She did not give me her sickness after all, and while I have remained healthy, I bonded my spirit and thought with this young mother who had a smiling child, and who, in those days, was destined for a tragic ending.

At times, absurdly, I feel as if my blood is mixed with hers, wondering whether her passing away was painful and prolonged as if I could picture her death. And during those times when I feel her blood mingling with mine, I often light a candle in a darkened room hoping that the light will reach her wherever she may be. And then, I say a prayer for Kim, my sister in blood.

Obsession

In a dream, Joan sees him together with his wife in some kind of a communal home. It has large rooms with sparse furniture and it is nondescript and confusing as things often appear in dreams. Joan is talking to friends and acquaintances that are collected there, in this nondescript home, and she seems to be happy and pleased to be among people.

She sees him there and it does not disturb her. She talks loudly and laughs heartily, and the two of them, she and David, politely talk to each other. Then his wife begins her talk in a strange language, and Joan wonders if the language is perhaps Portuguese.

"Why Portuguese?" she thinks to herself, since the wife is not Portuguese.

But then, the wife suddenly turns to Joan and speaking in a non-accented English, invites her to come with them.

Where?

The wife is pleasant and cheerful as someone secure in herself. Secure in her position. Secure in her marriage. Joan thinks that she is condescending and patronizing. Joan walks through this household, through many rooms full of people, and her chest is bare. Her breasts are exposed, but she just walks through, ignoring everyone, alone, self-centered, angry.

There is not much reaction to her rebellion, and no one seems to be overly concerned about her bare chest. The wife is seated watching her with not too much interest. Joan thinks of herself as passé. She is not consequential.

When she wakes up, her dream seems so real that she continues to be angry and defeated, the sweat soaking her hair and her

33

nightgown.

The memory of David.

"Why does he still disturb me?"

She did everything to forget. She left the University, her teaching position, her research and the publishing of her work, when they split. Far from the University she lives now in a small provincial town, and works sporadically, substituting in different local high schools. She had organized her life around trivial things and hoped that in this way she could easily forget.

And now this dream.

The dream repeats itself with a woman in it, her face serene, her language pseudo-Portuguese becoming suddenly American-English and David, Joan's ex-lover is there, himself also serene, watching his woman. Belonging. They both belong to each other. She, Joan, is the outsider.

Joan wakes up sweating. Her head is hurting, her muscles are rigid. It is the middle of the night and the thermos bottle on the night table has coffee in it. She takes the pill, has a sip of coffee and tries to go back to sleep. In the morning she thinks that she has to get rid of the dream. It is hurting her, exhausting her, making it difficult for her to continue everyday life. The dream makes her angry at him, his wife, and the world. Perhaps, she should find him. He still teaches at the same University. Should she go and see him? Should she face him, talk to him, attack him?

Joan is not violent. She would like to just abolish all these years of their separate lives. To start all over and continue as it was before. But there is the woman. Could we abolish the woman?

She wishes for another dream. A dream in which she gets rid of the woman that is her obstacle. Destroy her in a non-violent manner. Make her disappear as if she never existed. Is there some magic way to do it? During the day she tries to compose herself and run her chores. She tries to keep a ledger, a diary, a memoir.

Her friend Louise knows all about Joan's troubled life. Louise teaches in the local school where Joan works occasionally as a substitute teacher. They have, at times, lunch together in a small café where sandwiches, coffee and tea is served. There is no rush in that place, so they can sit and talk for pretty long periods of time. Joan's other friends from the University have all abandoned her. No one wishes to communicate with her. How could she abandon everything that she has achieved, her whole career because of a man? Joan knows that they have abandoned her. Louise is her only support group. Louise sits with her in the coffee shop and finds her looking tired. Joan has more wrinkles on her fair skin than a week before and her hair is curling unevenly around her face. They sip their coffee and Louise asks her:

"Are you tired?"

"Sort of," she answers, "I don't sleep well these days."

"Why?" Louise asks but she already knows. Joan is thinking of David. Off and on, she resuscitates the whole, sorry past. She then does not work and does not take care of herself. By not having a steady job, letting her hair grow ungroomed and wearing dark glasses, she hides herself from the world.

David wrote to her just a month before she was to leave her post overseas, where she was spending a year working on her PhD thesis. A letter that she just could not accept. He wrote a letter. Not a phone call, or an e-mail. A typed letter from his computer, totally impersonal. In it, he said that he had found another woman with whom he was very much in love. He was going to marry her. He was sorry that it ended this way. He wished her all the best in her life and in her career. Surely, she would find happiness in the future with someone else.

Such a stupid, trite letter. So common place. After years of togetherness, to throw on her such banalities. What happened? One year of distance to destroy years of being together.

It was painful to think. It was painful to live. David ought to be dead. This way Joan would perhaps heal.

Louise looks at her and tells her:

"Why don't you forget? There is life after David, Joan."

Only if he is dead, Joan thinks, but she does not say it aloud.

Could a dream kill? She thinks of what Louise had said and tries to compose herself.

She will try to compose herself. She will try to go back to teaching full time in another place, or in another city. Joan sends her résumé with a letter to different institutions in different cities. Her résumé is impressive, and her credentials superior. But she was absent for six years now and wondering whether any institution would be interested.

She would have to wait.

This is what she tells Louise on her next get-together. But Louise is not convinced. Joan looks dreadful. Her eyes are puffy, her hair unwashed, tied with a ribbon on the back of her head carelessly. Wisps of hair escape from the knot falling out on her cheeks. They eat their vegetarian sandwich and drink their coffee.

Louise says:

"You should go back and talk to him. See him in order to clear this from your mind. It has been almost seven years and things change. It could be different. Hop on the train and ask him to have a cup of coffee with you. In the cafeteria. In the University. This is where it all started, this is where it should end."

They take a walk together, look at the stores, buy stuff. Then each goes to their cars, Louise back to her husband and children and Joan to her apartment.

Joan reflects on Louise's words about going to the University, seeing him and talking. She is forcing herself to think. Will she do it? Yes, she will. She calls Louise to tell her that she will take a train. It is easier than driving, thus avoiding a change of mind. Boarding Amtrak she goes to the city where they had spend so much time together—working, researching, helping each other, living together, making love, being happy. Will David want to see her? He still teaches at the same University that she never went back to. The short trip on Amtrak makes her remember.

Arriving into the city she did not see in about seven years makes her nervous and insecure. She remembers a motel close to the school and stops there to collect her thoughts and her courage. Looking in the mirror she sees herself as if for the first time in years. She looks presentable in her new suit. Her hair is orderly, done in a beauty parlor with curls distributed nicely around her face with a light makeup that makes her wrinkles less pronounced. She looks elegant and almost beautiful. After having a cup of coffee in the coffee shop she returns to her room. Finally, she dials the number knowing that at one o'clock in the afternoon David is most likely in his office.

David's voice comes over the wire, the "hallo" that she recognized instantly.

There is a second of silence then Joan says:

"David, this is Joan."

Another split second of silence and Joan hears David say:

"Hallo Joan, where are you?"

"I am here in town, David. David, I want to see you. Please."

His voice is cautious, almost tinged with fear:

"Are you here to see me, or do you plan to work here?"

"No David. I just want to see you and to talk to you. I do not plan any unpleasantness. I will return back tomorrow morning with the first train available."

"Let's meet in the dining room and talk over a cup of coffee."

"What time David?"

"Within an hour Joan. Do you need transportation?"

"No David. I'm nearby."

"Well then, within an hour."

She prepares herself and looking in the mirror realizes that she has lost quite a bit of weight. Being a close distance from the University, she decides to walk, perhaps also to prolong the moment when she would have to face David. The streets are like old friends, known to her, making her feel almost at home. Same gates to the buildings and to the grounds through which she has past innumerable times in "her previous life." Joan looks for flowers and sees the same white and pink Impatiens around the tree skirts and the trees casting shadows on the walks where she is going toward the known building.

She thinks: *Am I doing this? Am I really here? Did time stop or am I still dreaming in my own bed?*

But she is walking toward the building in which she knows is David's office. Through the heavy doors, at the entrance, the big staircase is facing her and on both sides of the atrium are the elevators. People walk back and forth, rushing, trying to reach some important destination. She takes the elevator to the second floor, and finds the door with David's name in it. She has been there before.

Time has stopped.

Joan knocks on the door and enters without waiting to be asked to come in. David is sitting at his desk with books piled on one side and different papers on the other. A series of computers are on one long table taking almost one whole wall, while on the opposite side are the bookshelves.

Are there pictures? Joan thinks as she looks around the room. *Wife, children?*

David gets up from behind the desk and walks toward her:

"Joan," he says, "Joan." He takes her hand in both of his and smiles. His face is more rotund, his cheeks are pink, and he looks like an elderly cherub. Joan has a terrible need to laugh aloud.

He is overweight.

They look at each other for a moment and then he says:

"Shall we go to the dining room and have a sandwich?"

She nods silently and they walk together to the elevator. There are other people on the elevator that Joan does not know, and they exchange small talk with David.

She watches his overweight body, his cherub face and thinks: *Is this David?* Only the eyes are the same, but covered with heavy eyelids appearing smaller and more distant.

The Cafeteria is bustling with people coming in and out. Students, professors, adjuncts. Sitting at the table in the corner, she observes all this and remembers. It brings back memories of work with the students, dialogs with colleagues.

"I just want a cup of coffee," she says.

David will have a sandwich and a coffee. Big sandwich. He munches on his sandwich, heartily with almost sexual pleasure.

Oral gratification, Joan thinks drinking her coffee. All of a sudden she has nothing to say to David. This strange man is not her ex-boyfriend. She only wants to leave.

"You did not change much," David says.

"But you did," she answers and they both laugh. He knows that he looks different.

"How is your wife?"

"She is okay. She teaches at the local high school." "Mathematics," he adds.

"Only okay?" she asks and he does not answer.

"Joan," he asks, "How are you doing? Did you get married? Do you have a friend?"

"No, David. After you left me I isolated myself pretty much from everything. And everyone."

"I'm sorry, Joan," he says and she thinks: *Is this a cliché or is this for real?*

"I am glad that I was able to see you again. You know, David, I had to close this chapter forever, so that I may get on with my life." *And with my work*, she thinks to herself.

"And did you close it?"

"It is closed as of today," she answers.

He looks at her, and this time she thinks that his regret is real.

"I am truly sorry. But it was good to see you."

"David, I have to go. I am catching the train tonight. Thank you for this visit. Too little time to talk anymore. Everybody here is rushing so." Joan says, observing the coming and going of people.

David takes care of the check and they both prepare to leave. They walk together to the exit and David says:

"I am going to walk you to the gate."

They walk among the trees and the flowers on the narrow walkway just as they did so many times before. At the gate they shake hands. David bends and kisses her hand. There is little of old David in that gesture, and she cringes slightly. But then she says:

"Thanks for the coffee and your company. I will walk now. It is a beautiful day."

"Yes it is," he says and she walks.

Is it possible that she feels so light, so exhilarated by the walk, the brisk air and the smell of ozone? She is human again. *I did want him dead*, Joan thinks. *What a nasty, ugly thought.* She smiles at people she is passing by and they smile in return. Joan will be home this evening and will call Louise to tell her that all is well. In the days to come, she will look forward to hear about her résumé. It is a great résumé. Surely, some college would want to hire her.

Jenny

I am lying in my bed in the nursing home and I don't think I shall leave this bed anymore. I am very thin and my bones have diminished in volume. My skin and muscles are stuck together in an uneven pattern. I look like a medium size doll. My dentures don't fit and my hands are crippled by arthritis.

I am a monster doll.

My daughter comes regularly to visit me and sometimes I acknowledge her presence, but sometimes I don't. I fix the scarf around her neck as I used to do when she was a young girl, and it brings tears to her eyes. I restrain myself since I don't want her to be unhappy. The time for tears has long gone.

At times, I drift into semi-consciousness and then I see her from a great distance where she reminds me of myself when I was younger and healthier.

She has my features, and she smiles showing the perfect set of white teeth as I once had; it seems that I see myself again in her as I used to be before old age and disease devastated my body. Before leaving, she always adjusts my pillow, combs my hair and puts an afghan, neatly folded, on the bottom of my bed.

Once, I was blond and blue-eyed, which my daughter is not since her father was a dark Irishman. I was eighteen years old when I took him home to meet my grandmother. My grandmother had brought me up. Both of my parents had died when I was a little girl. They had died a few months apart from each other, stricken by an influenza epidemic that was ravaging the country at the time. I was told that my father had loved my mother so much that he simply could not live without her. This story was very strange to me. Perhaps I did not count.

My grandmother did not approve of my choice. "You are too young to marry," she had said, "and this man is a fortune hunter." But I was taken by his handsome darkness and we eloped.

We had a great time together. I still remember our weekends spent at the shore, driving the fanciest of cars and dancing the nights away. But it did not last—we had to settle down eventually. Soon after, my daughter was born. Then, one day, he left when it was getting obvious that the money might not last forever.

Did I miss him? He must be dead by now since he was older than I was. I never tried to find him, not even for my child. Strange, when I think of it today, how could I have let him disappear so suddenly? I can still see his smiling face, his shock of dark hair, his handsomeness—and yet, I don't remember missing him.

It was such a long time ago.

I had my daughter then, and my grandmother took us both back. Grandmother was not a very talkative person. She did not say, "I told you so." She was not very demonstrative either; no hugs and kisses, no small talk in the parlor while crocheting or listening to the radio. But her sense of duty never left her and when she died, she left my daughter and me reasonably well off.

My daughter was a beautiful little girl. I would dress her up exquisitely and we would go to children's Easter parades on the boardwalk in Atlantic City. She would always get the first prize. There was something oddly reassuring in this.

My girl. I can safely say I wasn't a suffocating mother, and neither was I a victim. To me, she was life—a sense of wellness and happiness, the very essence of what makes life worth living and liking.

She was so beautiful and when she grew up and got married, her children were beautiful also. I always made sure that I gave them great presents for their birthdays and for holidays—extravagant presents that cost lots of money. They loved me; they loved their presents; and they loved themselves. And so we lived for a time.

These days, when I am lying in this borrowed bed and when I can think clearly, I wonder whether we had put too much emphasis on physical beauty. I dare to wonder whether a part of our inner strength had withered and died like a plant that wasn't watered sufficiently. It is a pity. Now, the time has passed, and now, it's all the same. And now is no longer the time for thinking and worrying.

My illness started insidiously and it was a strange one. No doctor ever diagnosed me correctly. At first, when I was in my sixties perhaps, it seemed that it was my heart. I would start with heart palpitations and was rushed to the hospital each time by my apprehensive daughter. Each time I was given many medications.

I took them all. I wanted to be well. At least, I think I wanted to be well. After these incidents, a strange anxiety would suddenly overcome me and I would be unable to breathe. I would feel as if I was on the brink of death and may at any moment die right then and there in front of everyone.

This was terrifying and embarrassing at the same time. I was disrupting my daughter's and her children's lives. The children were grown by now, and coming and going. I would wait in my home for them to appear and to spend time with me, so that I could enjoy their youthfulness and be a part of their lives. But, in time, I saw them less and less.

Then my gait became unstable; my knees began to give way. I kept telling myself it was nothing. I even began to exercise a little. But I fell a few times, not being able to keep my balance.

My daughter was traveling with her husband at the time and when she came home she found me in a hospital with a fractured hip. I healed eventually, but I could not move about freely and I was afraid of falling further. I walked slowly and held myself up by grasping furniture.

I needed assistance and could not live alone anymore. Throughout my life, I spent money freely and foolishly and had little left for my old age. But, I did not need much. I hoped that my daughter would take me into her household and that we would be close together in my last years, for our love of each other and for my love of her children. But she could not do it. She said that it would not be fair to her husband. She also said that taking care of me would become a

43

physical burden to her and might even ruin her own health.

I began to shrink more quickly now. My hands then started to clench into spasms and the fingers became so distorted that I could not open my palms.

The nursing home into which they put me was not too bad. The room was clean and my daughter brought me a beautifully colored afghan to put at the bottom of my bed to keep my feet warm. It was a patchwork of pastel patterns, similar to those you see in Monet paintings. When she would come, I could see a terror in her face hidden behind smiles and talk of what her family was doing and what she was planning for the week.

Whenever she came, she would harass the nursing staff with her constant questions and complaints, especially when she would find my food untouched on my night table. Many times I could not eat my lunch or supper and nobody would care much—after all, there were so many of us, old and frail, and to the nurses and kitchen aides, we were all the same. There was no special time to waste on improving my eating habits.

When I was able to get out of bed, she would take me in a wheelchair into the garden of the nursing home and sometimes make me laugh, but I was becoming less and less responsive and more of my lunches were left untouched.

"Would you want me to bring you something from home?" my daughter would ask as she removed the untouched food—and I know she was protesting with the staff, but they did not pay any great attention to her.

I spoke less and less and would only shake my head as an answer.

She would bring candy and chocolate that I would not eat; she would comb my hair and cut my nails, and then leave with a promise to come back—she had so many duties and obligations at home.

The last time I left this bed was to be moved to a hospital when my body was totally emaciated. I was twisted and distorted, and my skin was hanging in large folds off my bones. I was to be hydrated and put back in shape so that I could return back to the nursing home.

Everybody came to see me: my daughter with her husband, my

granddaughters with their husbands or respective boyfriends. They all came and went except my youngest granddaughter, who was not in town. But I was told that she was soon returning and that the first thing she would do would be to come and see me. That gave me great pleasure and I waited patiently for her while they were fluffing the pillow, uneasily watching IV fluids running into my veins and then finally retiring to their comfortable homes.

In the hospital bed my mind was slowly going. My body was full of sore spots where the pressure of the bones against the bedding was too much for my poor skin.

At some time, I thought of my grandmother and the husband who had never returned and how I had never found the need to look for him.

Who knows why things turn out the way they do?

In my lucid moments, I was waiting for my youngest granddaughter—my favorite—to come and see me. But when she finally came, I was already gone.

Remembrances

After a long absence M and R decided to take their children to the "Old Country." It was time for them to discover the traditions and the arts, and to enjoy the pristine shores of many Mediterranean inlets.

After a week or so, driving though the villages and the countryside, they stopped their wandering at a small, dainty hotel that was perched on a promontory above the Adriatic sea. There was a beach below and, on the autostrada in the back of the hotel, they were able to take their two children into the city. The green pine trees gradually descended on the steep ravine into the silvery blue water. Looking though the descending greenery, M. envisioned the hanging gardens of the seven wonders in the ancient world and imagined herself as possibly living in them in those days, a long, long time ago.

Sitting on the terrace of the hotel in the morning and looking at the vastness of the sea, smelling the herbs and the marigolds, she envisioned the scenes from Maxwell Parish paintings, his ladies sitting on the balustrade, surrounded by the flowers, watching the sun rising in the distance.

Fantasy. Myth.

She loved both. The world of fantasy was perhaps a reality. At times she doted on it, forgetting the rest, even if only for a very small fraction of time.

On the terrace a sculpture of the Greek God Pan was standing in its own niche. A nude body with thin long arms and legs holding an instrument that reminded M. of the Irish bagpipes.

Reality and fantasy lived in her on those sunny days in the dainty little hotel with a beach below.

They would take their two children into the city to the ancient monuments and the big old churches, trying to introduce them to the world of art and not succeeding very well. The children, a boy of seven and a girl of nine years enjoyed the water more, where small boats would take them around cruising close to the shore. They would try to fish and collect dark mussel shells which they would fling back into the water. They would save only a few, so they could show their important findings to their parents.

A beautiful summer. Sitting on the beach for part of the day, sunning, not worrying about melanomas and keratosis. M. and R. were still young, perhaps somewhat ignorant, and not yet indoctrinated into prevention and health hazards. It was marvelous to be able to worship the sun.

On one such sunny day, sitting in her beach chair, M. spotted her. The face was unusual: a thin perfect nose with flared nostrils as if she were always short of breath. A young face and yet not so young. Nice body, well built, getting somewhat matronly. Next to her an older husband with gray hair and brilliant blue eyes.

Sailor's eyes.

Or German eyes.

M. was sure that she knew this woman from somewhere. Those flared nostrils, on very white skin and dark hair, were definitely familiar. She watched her in the dining room and when passing by each other they would both smile as people usually do when staying at the same hotel. There was no sign that she recognized M.

One day, M. approached her and asked: "Do I know you from somewhere?"

"O yes," she said, "we saw each other on the beach." She and her husband smiled happily. There was no recognition, and M. left it at that.

It took M. a few days to remember. When she finally did, it was as if she went back many years, into another world, into another time. A time when they were classmates and the war was raging through old Europe.

M. was glad and happy for her that she was prosperous and alive.

They met again in the parking lot of the hotel going out into the city. M. observed her in her elegant afternoon dress, short dark hair, good makeup. She bore not a trace of the frivolous new world of the late sixties.

She was standing in the parking lot, waiting for her husband to pull the car out so she could comfortably step into a big 220-S Mercedes Benz with an automatic shift and air conditioning, initial "D" for Deutschland. M. looked at her own rental, a 120 Fiat also with automatic shift and air and thought that both had fared reasonably well by average standards. M. even felt a twinge of envy for her extremely calm elegance and conservative aura.

Watching her in the parking lot, it made M. think. She wondered what happened to so many young people who had survived those far away days. Far away years. And she thought that, after so many years, perhaps it did not matter. It did not matter to the ones that survived. The survivors learned to forget and forgive, and also learned to be forgotten and forgiven. They dispersed and started all over again with new personas and new outlooks on life. Their children did not learn about their plights, their loves and hatreds. Their sacrifices. Their crimes. Slowly but surely, there was a loss of perspective and the issues became more and more confused. And then, the issues did not exist any more. The causes became obsolete to all, except for the ones who had died for them. And the dead could not talk.

The dead.

The dead minded still, very much. Every once in a while they would protest the complacency of the survivors. There were too many graves to be forgotten. Single graves, common graves. Undug graves and some that nobody knew about.

They protested, but not much attention was to be given.

And the women? "Le vierges ont pleuré longtemps."

Women wept, then stopped the weeping. Some married much older men, some much younger. Some even married those who should have been their enemy. They even met in a parking lot of a small hotel on a summer day without recognizing each other.

****

Sitting on the beach or going into town, a good looking woman in a Mercedes, driven by a handsome man, with a gentle face, a white mane of hair—and brilliant blue eyes.

****

The children threw the fish and the mussels back into the water. A last swim, a last listening to the silent music of the Greek deity, the Pan, playing his Irish bagpipes. And then, time to go back home.

Martha and Her Dogs

During her long illness, when she spent long hours in the stillness of her bedroom, Martha thought not only about her children but also about the dogs that they had owned during their life together.

Years ago, while driving with her daughter Diana, on the Parkway, they saw a German Shepherd running through the traffic among the speeding cars that crowded the highway. Lost, obviously abandoned by his people at the end of the summer season, it seemed as if he was looking for a fast car to put an end to it all.

"It seems as if he is trying to commit suicide," said Diana.

Impulsively, Martha said, "Please, let's stop and pick him up."

But Diana had always had a lot of good common sense: "It is impossible to stop in this traffic, Mother. Besides, we don't know whether he would trust us or not. He could possibly even attack us."

Martha knew that Diana was right. There was nothing they could do for the dog. They continued their journey in silence, thinking the same thought: the dog did not care whether he lived or died.

Then there was another German Shepherd in their lives. The children's father had brought the puppy when the children were growing, and the puppy grew up to be a big, beautiful dog they named Wolf.

Wolf loved the children and both parents. Martha's mother was living with them then, and running the household—and Wolf loved her, too. But he did not like anyone else. No amount of training, coaxing or chastising made Wolf like or tolerate anyone who might come to the door—delivery boys, merchants, family friends.

Whenever the doorbell rang, he would go to the door and bark and snarl and no begging or threatening would make him leave the door and let people in. He was a big dog. And though the children could ride him or pull his ears, no stranger could get into the house. It became necessary to lock him away in the basement each time someone was at the door. The grandmother had to watch for the delivery boy, the vegetable man and the garbage collectors—people whom Wolf would not tolerate and would show all signs of wanting to attack in order to protect the family.

It happened one day that the person delivering the dry cleaning came and the grandmother had forgotten to lock Wolf in the basement. While she was talking to the man, Wolf came into the hallway and leaped to attack the stranger, his bared teeth visible to both the grandmother and the dry cleaner. In desperation, the grandmother stepped in front of the dog and put her hand into his open jaw. Wolf stopped; he did not close his mighty jaw on the grandmother's hand. By that time, the man had hidden quickly in the guest closet. The grandmother somehow managed to take Wolf and lock him away in the cellar. The dry cleaner and the grandmother shook hands, and the man, shaken, thanked her profusely for saving his life.

After this episode, Wolf spent more and more time in the basement. Martha often wondered what went through his head while he was roaming the dark, dank basement that everyone in the household avoided.

Martha's husband was the only one who could take him for a walk, and sometimes he and the children did just that. Wolf was so big and beautiful, such a perfect specimen of his species. And on one such occasion, while he was being walked, Wolf decided to dart across the street to get to the children who were playing at the time in the front yard. He was so strong—it was impossible to restrain him. He ran right in front of a car that was turning the corner of the usually quiet street and was struck by it. He was struck dead. Everybody cried. Everybody cried for weeks.

Wolf was buried in the backyard, deep in the ground, and the grass grew over his grave. It was their big secret; for a long time the children visited his grave regularly each day. Everybody in the house now hated the basement. No one would go there since the death of

Wolf—but the cleaning had to be done.

So the basement was cleaned and painted and the pain of the loss slowly went away.

Then the time came to leave the big house with the large basement. The family was disintegrating. Martha and her husband separated after many years. Her mother had gone to live with her other daughter. She passed away just before Martha moved from the old house.

Martha bought a smaller house for herself and the children. But this house was not a happy one. It was perched on top of a small hill and during the winter months the driveway was always so frozen that the car had to be kept on the street. The backyard would also become full of ice and the back door could be opened only after cutting through the ice with some sharp tool. The cold of the winter was making everyone in the house rigid and hostile, and the children would be taciturn in the morning on the way to the school bus.

Times were difficult in the unfriendly house, where the air was stale and the smell of cooking was everywhere. Into this atmosphere of gloom, Cuddles came to live with them.

Diana had said to her mother, "Mom, I want a dog. I want my own dog."

For a few days, they looked through the newspapers where the ads for acquiring a pet were published. They chose one puppy—that one for no particular reason—and wanted to see him.

They telephoned the owners and the next day a man and a woman—husband and wife—came to the house carrying a small dog, soft and fluffy, with white and yellow spots.

Diana said, "I will call him Cuddles." The name that his owners had given him was different, but Diana never used it and it was soon forgotten.

The people who brought Cuddles were a kind couple who evidently loved the dogs they bred. They gave them some instructions on how to take care of the dog and, after being paid, left the puppy with Martha and the children.

The children made a bed for him in the bathroom with old towels and gave him milk and some dog biscuits. The poor little puppy cried all night; they could not calm him at all. Thinking back, Martha wondered how much he must have suffered missing his mother and the rest of the litter that were not with him anymore. But at that time, they thought this was the way it should be—that all puppies cried and carried on until they got used to their new owners.

Eventually he did get used to them and love them, but that night he cried pitifully for a long time, locked in the children's bathroom where they had made a makeshift bed for him with old towels. In the morning, Martha found him exhausted and asleep on his makeshift bed, and around him on the bathroom floor were scattered many little brown objects. She thought her son, David, had been playing with his army soldiers and had left them there on the floor. Instead, the puppy Cuddles had his "duty" all over the bathroom floor, except on the bedding where he had finally fallen asleep, lonely and exhausted after his crying spell. The children laughed when they saw the "false" lead soldiers on the floor, and Martha had laughed with them. For a long time, they remembered that first morning and their first episode with Cuddles. The laughter they shared was the first gift that Cuddles gave them.

From a soft, fluffy puppy, Cuddles grew to be a medium-sized, adult English Setter with white and orange fur and a wonderful disposition. Although the house was considered oppressive, the neighborhood was not. The neighborhood was full of dogs, children, and busy mothers. Cuddles spent a large amount of his time outdoors always in the neighborhood running with the children and dogs, always returning home in the evening to be with the family. Then he would go to his bed in the basement, which was quite different from the basement where poor Wolf was forced to spend most of his time. It was a pleasant room with carpeted floors and paneled walls with shelves full of books that no one was reading. He was able to come up to the first floor anytime through an open gate that led into the kitchen, and he would do this and lie on the steps, taking a nap after an active day. When the children were home from school on the weekend, he would stay home with them.

Cuddles was a kind and patient dog. He accepted the children's sometimes rough playing with tolerance and good humor. While lying in bed, it would bring tears to Martha eyes remembering the children laughingly recounting how they used to pull his tail at times. It had to be painful, but then she would see a happy dog greeting her when she came home from work, who was not paying much attention to the children's rough play.

When Cuddles was ten years old, they moved to another house, one that was full of light and had big, spacious rooms, a kitchen they all liked, and an enclosed yard that was accessible through the kitchen door. Cuddles was able to run through the yard, and, in the evening, there was no basement for him to live in. He would sleep in the kitchen and in the morning would wait to be taken for a walk and then for a run.

On top of the stairs leading to the upper floor, he would often sleep through the afternoons. When the children—now adults—moved away to live in dormitories at different colleges, Martha was left alone. She remained in the big house and Cuddles was her friend. Time stole most of her memories of those moments with him. She remembered his presence as something abstract, benevolent—almost spiritual. She was alone but did not feel alone.

Cuddles developed a habit of sleeping on the carpet next to Martha's bed. And early in the morning, he would start walking through the room making a persistent tapping noise until she would get up. She would get dressed and let him into the yard through the kitchen door. The early morning air would be invigorating, and she would become wide-awake. She was feeling healthy, and this did not present a hardship to her.

As the years were slipping away, Diana and David would come home periodically and Cuddles was always there to greet them. It seemed as if he was looking forward to their visits. But their visits were getting further apart, and Martha and Cuddles were getting older.

Cuddles started to walk through the house during the night, up and down the stairs, and Martha found it difficult to sleep. She would get up in the middle of the night and take him into the yard and let him run, hoping that he would become exhausted and go back to sleep on the carpet in the bedroom. But it was to no avail. He would continue his walk through the house, restlessly, as if having severe insomnia.

Then Cuddles stopped eating. He became very thin and did not look pretty. He was no longer the dog that was admired when he was outdoors with his white and orange fur and playful disposition. He became restless and remote. The vet could not find any disease, and the diagnosis was "old age" and "cachexia." Did he miss the children or the house where he could roam with other dogs on the cul-de-sac street? Or was he just becoming too old to care any more?

Martha and Cuddles just lost each other. Cuddles did not want to live anymore. The little food that he ate he could not digest, and the house was becoming filled with the foul smell of vomit and diarrhea.

So one day she took him in her arms to the vet and asked the vet to put him to sleep. She walked home alone, lost and totally numb. David and Diana came home and collected his ashes. They dispersed them among the flowerbeds near the fence in the back yard, where he used to run in the early mornings with Martha watching him.

She never forgave herself for letting him go. She would reprimand herself for not putting up with his cachexia and lack of energy, and for not nurturing him until the end came to him naturally and possibly without pain. But that was not the case. He was put to sleep on the stainless steel table in the veterinary office—the ultimate rejection and the ultimate treachery.

A very young artist had painted a picture of Cuddles from a photograph that David had taken of him while he was resting peacefully on top of the staircase, taking his afternoon nap. In the painting, he was in the hallway, beautiful and healthy. Martha would stop often, looking at it, and many times crying alone would ask in a loud voice: "How could I have done this to you? How could I?"

And, of course, he did not answer.

The Shadow Mom*

It is a true obsession that I have to think about this woman whom I have not seen for some years. She has nowadays an immense power in her country, and uses it ruthlessly against those who are contrary to her ruling party and to her family. She maintains a low profile and holds no office, while others hold positions of authority and carry titles. Her personal office is still full of pictures of fallen tyrants. She considers herself a follower of theirs, and within the power structure in which she has ascended, she deems this not to be a contradiction. What would seem to be a contradiction to different people in different countries does not seem so to her at all.

When she gets out of her office and into the city that once upon a time had all the trappings of a modern metropolis, goons who carry heavy guns and walk the swaggering walk of strongmen soon surround her.

She herself walks slowly and with grace. Her long thick mane is orderly. Her shoes with not-too-high heels give her the bourgeois look of a housewife. At times, she likes to appear as such, pretending to be simple, vulnerable, domesticated. At times, I suspect she herself believes this to be so.

She is the mother of four sons, grown up and spoiled by her. Four sons, that in the world of tyranny and corruption, among famine and unemployment, drive Ferraris, dress in Armani, and play tennis regularly.

She did not raise her sons properly. But then, thinking of her own childhood, she may have had the need to be overindulgent, and thus allowed them to grow up without discipline or responsibility. And

without honor.
Is this what she fought for?
It is hard to say.
It is hard to be a woman.

Our first meeting was by chance, in my young days, when I was wandering through places in search for answers, reading books and looking the world up. We met on a narrow Mediterranean beach in late summer when the tourists were all but gone. The water, emerald green and transparent, mirroring the bottom covered with stones of various sizes with an occasional sea urchin and small water creatures jumping like miniature horses in the transparency of the sea. At a distance, the sea would change from green to different shades of blue, heavy with salt, hugging our bodies, making them light, embracing us like a mother would embrace a child. We would get out when its salty content would make our eyes red and our skin dry and wrinkled. When we would get out of the water, a small wind would keep our bodies cool and dry our hair. It was a beautiful late summer.

We started to talk to each other easily, discussing the beauty of the place and then, talking about books, literature and poetry. At that time, my fascination was with the Russians, and I was avidly reading Dostoyevski, wallowing in his characters who were half demons, half saints, and his heroines all sacrificing and stoically tolerating their misfortunes (the ones who did not do so usually succumbing to tragic ends). Other tragic heroes were also on my list: Jessenin, Majakovski, Maxim Gorki. She, although familiar with my heroes, was into French literature, having an interest in Chateaubriand, Lamatine and even Verlain.

What a twist of fate: so many years after, I am small in my endeavors, living in American suburbia, still enjoying good books, but deeply removed from the great Russian classics, while my distant friend has become only a distant memory to me.

And then, one day, by accident, I read in a national magazine some excerpts from her biography; small fragments, like footnotes about who she was and how it all began. I vividly remembered then her sitting on the narrow beach, sunning herself on a big rock, speaking of Lamartine.

She was conceived somewhere in the mountains where both of her parents were freedom fighters. She was born there, surely no place for a newborn child, and given to family and friends to care for her, and place where she could be protected. After that, the story became obscure and murky with no clear picture of the three of them as a family. One thing is certain—they all survived the horrors of war. The father became an important person, an organizer in the newly formed governing body and then fade out slowly as did many others. He never cared for her—his little girl, even to the point of abandonment.

The story of her mother is even more twisted and murky, with rumors of treachery, imprisonment, torture and death. Who were the torturers? Who the executioners? Her own people, perhaps? Those she had fought with for freedom? She died in prison of an unnatural death, either by execution or after sustaining repeated torture. How many women have perished in a similar manner, ostracized, accused of strange crimes, abandoned by the mainstream, reverted from being heroes into ridicule, obscurity even death? It happened to many of them.

While in prison waiting to be judged, she spent her time knitting small outfits for her daughter—booties, a little hat, a little pink sweater...

Meanwhile, the little girl was living among relatives, abandoned by her father with an absent mother who was knitting a little pink sweater for her—the never-seen child-daughter. According to the biographer, the grown-up daughter, the powerful gray eminence, still preserves and treasures those hand-made items as mementos of her tragic unknown mother. What thought, what feeling may a growing child harbor who was conceived so cruelly, abandoned by an unloving father, and collecting little mementos of a mother who was unable to hug her and see her grow into adulthood?

After reading this, I have cried for her, whom I have not seen in years, for the pain and loss she must have suffered, and out of which perhaps she has emerged cruel and unfeeling.

I grieved each time I remembered.

I grieved for her, whenever I thought of her and blamed my lack of logic and my mushy over-sentimentalism. But I could not help myself.

I met her again on a summer day in the city where everyone considers her to be the one who moves the strings attached to the backs of the governing bureaucrats with a pretense of democracy when in truth there is absolutism and an old-fashioned tyranny.

We met in a charming little café on the bank of the vast and lazy river that touches the city, she being well protected on all sides by bodyguards. No meetings for her in hotel lounges or restaurants, since many assassinations have been executed in open spaces where diplomats and journalists come and go freely, and a handful of courageous tourists may also wander in looking for adventure and news. The café is more intimate and safe, and she obviously did not want to stay too long.

She agreed to talk with me because of that distant time when we had met and spoken, both in love with the sea, the salty breezes, and the smell of rosemary and wild mint.

We drank Turkish coffee, dipping sugar cubes in it, and I looked at her: differently….a stranger.

"It has been a long time," I said, opening the conversation with such a trivial statement. "I am glad to see you again."

Her smile was a bit artificial and perhaps a trifle condescending.

"I see that you are traveling. Still in love with the salty water and the sunny Mediterranean?"

"It will always be my first love," I said.

I remembered what I had read about her; of her present and of her past, and I tried to reach out to her in my thoughts, hoping to alleviate the burden she was carrying, which was perhaps making her be what she had become. I couldn't help but love her and cry for her (albeit inwardly) there, in that secluded little café, where she was surrounded by her scruffy bodyguards.

I have cried each time I have remembered this woman, who was born tragically out of broken dreams, out of heroic myths. The myths were transformed into trash and misery, and she became ruthless, cold and unforgiving. And ultimately self-destructing.

"Do you still have the little pink jacket your Mom knitted for you?" I had to ask.

She was quiet for a while, looking at me, thinking, pondering why I would ask such a question of her.

I asked my question *sottovoce,* almost whispering, afraid that tears might start rolling down my face.

She leaned over the table to touch my hand.

"Yes, I still have it," she said. "I have no daughters, so no one will inherit it."

And suddenly, she spoke to me intimately as if we were sitting together on that distant beach.

"It's hard to be a woman."

"Do you still read Lamartine?" I asked to break the spell between us. She laughed aloud and said:

"No more time for that."

"I have read your biography," I said to her "and felt it deeply as if it had happened to me."

Her look was distant and noncommittal.

"Thank you," she said. "Not many people feel such about me these days."

"Myself included," she said as an afterthought.

"Do you remember your Mom at all?" I asked and she answered promptly.

"No. I was an infant when Mother's relatives took me to live with them. I grew up in a large family and went to the university from there to become a lawyer."

It was time to leave. We got up. I spontaneously hugged her, although it perhaps was not the proper thing to do.

"I will pray for you," I said.

"I don't believe in God," she said smiling.

"It does not matter. God does not need to be acknowledged. I will pray for you."

We parted at that.

We both walked away from the little table in the café, each going our different ways; me disappearing into the crowds on the busy streets, anonymous, unknown; and she, surrounded by her protectors, returning to her palatial home on the hill.

* *Any similarity to people alive or dead is purely coincidental. This story is a total work of fiction.*

A Dangerous Summer

She had an agenda. Summer was approaching and her expectations were high. She was not in her prime, but she was strong and still had many goals to achieve. So many accomplishments scheduled. Her agenda was like a palette full of beautiful colors of autumn, vibrant and promising. So many books to read. So many letters to write, notes, stories, places to see, and thoughts to share.

She had an agenda. And it was shattered as if a shotgun hit a mirror and broke it into a thousand little pieces, broke it with a tremendous noise. So it started not as a deep sweet summer, with hot days, humidity, and abruptly sudden summer storms. Instead, it was the beginning of a dangerous summer.

She was diagnosed with a breast cancer. An area on her mammogram was vaguely abnormal. A very subtle irregularity, small not palpable, but on biopsy it was a cancer. Few millimeters in diameter but already invading the surrounding tissue and the lymph nodes.

The summer was stolen from her, she who had not many left.
The summer was to be filled with sadness, depression and anger.
Stolen summer.
Her via Crucis.

Further tests were done in cold, freezing rooms full of scanners. From one room to another she tolerated it all, stunned and unbelieving, walking into it like a somnambulist, asking herself the same question: how could this small, invisible tumor, hiding like a vicious little animal in a cave, be so invasive? The scans performed were reported negative but she had to have chemotherapy. And she was scheduled for it.

Weeping, and feeling betrayed. Weeping like the Guernica women did, their screams silent, mouths open, faces distorted. She wept in silence in her lonely home.

****

My first chemotherapy session, three agents, aggressive, working for cure. My oncologist explains it. I patiently let the treatment begin. I take a cold drink, chew on lollipops to avoid mouth sores. Few spots on my skin, red blotches but not permanent. Cramping, mild nausea. In three weeks I will have another treatment, and then, the whole blessed summer, every three weeks, anticipated tiredness, nausea and a head without hair.

Why am I so weepy? Why do I remember things long forgotten? The passing of seasons, the springs, the rain washing over bare limbs, arms strong, suntanned, hands with long fingers moving like a pianist's, umbrellas waving in the wind?

Is God out there, outside time, outside dimensions, waiting to give me a hand? Passing of time, passing of dimensions.

Please look at me.

Please hold my hand.

****

My hair is falling out, a sign that the Adriamycin is doing its job. There are a few hairs that are still clinging to my poor head. A few strands spread over my calvary like tufts of grass on an infertile ground. I go with a comb through it and throw them into a basket. I look into it as if accumulating some precious possessions.

My thin, ugly hair is disappearing. Collected into a bucket it is soft and fluffy and dead on arrival. No need for it anymore with Adriamycin flowing through my body.

Killing, killing, killing.

Healing, healing , healing.

The depression, the questioning, the lack of beauty. Is this also the part of healing? Is it a part of being alive, being able to feel, and being able to suffer?

Quod usque tandem dereliquisti me?

There is this indescribable feeling of need for something, for someone.

What is it? Who is it?

****

I feel as if my physical persona is disintegrating like a rotten vegetable or an overripe fruit that has lost the brilliance and the smoothness of its skin, the look of freshness.

Being alone with myself I have lost the power to talk to God. And perhaps I should talk. The poison that blotches my skin and tears my hair follicles is a cure. My oncologist tells me that it is a cure. And that it is possible that I am going to die of some other disease, but not of this abominable little cancer. Having said that, I still feel as if I don't belong to the human race. People around me that laugh, chat and make plans for lunch or the holiday meals, are like aliens to me. I am alone with my disease and condemned to spend half of my precious year in a recliner in the back if my sitting room, waiting for cure. And I should be grateful. I should be, but I am not.

I listen to my support group, the dear people that call me to offer love and assistance and I weep. Do I feel humiliated, because I am offered sympathy and help? What arrogance.

Help me, help me.

As time passes, my days are returning almost to normal. I am doing my regular chores. Like walking my dog, and breathing in the freshness of the early summer morning.

I watch myself with surprise in the mirror, and see my calvary so well sculpted, my face more visible and clear. My hair is starting to grow and is trying to become wavy, but not succeeding very well. Friends tell me that with a hat and a beret my face is fully exposed and it is beautiful. A few blotches show up on my body, and then disappear. When I am tired I close my eyes and inhale deeply. I silently pray without words.

At times, I am at peace.

****

While waiting for my fourth treatment, I am slightly anxious. Will I be sick again? Then I remember that the sickness disappears after two or three days and I am again without symptoms, able to go out, see places of interest to me.

My strength is coming back; my depression is lifting, although my mornings are still difficult. But this time I am talking and telling my oncologist that I have been depressed. My oncologist understands. It is normal with this treatment to be depressed. It will pass. "We are working for the cure here. This is not palliation. We are working for the cure." He prescribes an antidepressant and I take the prescription with me. I don't like pills. I don't like pills that mess up my brain. But I do need help this time, and I take the medicine.

At present I feel better. I can talk to my friends and family without weeping. I pray at times, silently, and talk to God in my thoughts. Not too often. Not yet.

Quod usque tandem-

****

I have to become humble. There are women who suffer from the same condition as mine.

Every seventh adult woman will develop the disease: a breast cancer. Why shouldn't I be a statistic? Don't I belong to a large community of adult women? I have to learn humility and accept the statistic.

As my oncologist says: "We are working for a cure."

For my next treatment I wait patiently. I know that after a few days I will stop having symptoms and will resume my every day life. I slowly replenish my spirit. It is a long road. It is my via Crucis.

I wear a hat, a beret, a kerchief. In the crowd, I am the only one that knows. This also will pass.

****

My treatment has been postponed, because my white cell count is lower than normal.
Also
—too many granulocytes.
My marrow, well hidden in the spongiosa of my bones, tucked in safety until Adriamycin and its other two colleagues came to visit.
So summer is going into a fall.
Give me my time.
Please, give me my time.
I should not complain. And I am not. I sit in my comfortable armchair, feeling somewhat tired and letting my bone marrow regenerate. I think that I am snapping out of my depression. I am accepting the fact that I have to offer my summer and part of the fall to the spirits of healing. I am letting my bone marrow work its way out of granulocytes. I will call my friends now and inform them of what is happening to my body. And to my spirit.

****

I am visiting my oncologist again, hoping that my marrow has regenerated enough, to accept Adriamycin and the other two of its colleagues.

I am being patient enough and I am waiting. I do not know what the day will bring. I am calm now, have been calm for a number of days. I should be grateful to the science, the times, and the survival statistics. And to the universe for being so kind, and in this awesome distress, offering me the possibility of healing.

Please, forgive me my trespasses.

****

My bone marrow has healed, and I am again in the hospital's oncology center. My vein is open, and a saline solution runs in smoothly. Then, one by one, the healers run into my vein, silently, with no fanfare. I think that I feel them coarsing through my blood stream, but it is only my imagination. All is proper, routine proper. The ominous is usually unassuming.

I have a few more treatments that make me somewhat sick for a few days with some nausea and cramping, and a general fatigue.

And then it passes.

I pick myself up and live my days. The trees are tall, and the leaves are changing their colors. They are swaying elegantly in the late summer breeze. I am told that I am a survivor.

My oncologist is upbeat, compassionate and supportive. He has walked with me, through the dangerous summer. He is one of the most accomplished in his field. His patients call him a saint.

****

She accepts the gift of life and picks her agenda again. Her face is beautiful. Her calvary is covered with soft, silver-white hair. Does she look radiant? Her friends think so.

There is so much to do. The summer is over.

Part II:
Notes and Missives from the
Windmill
(I am a wanderer)

Notes from the Windmill

The windmill reminds me a lot of a place my grandmother used to live in. It was located on the last floor of on old large building in the heart of the old city. The building was called "palazzo" because it was old and big, built like the others around it by *Her Majesty Maria Theresa, the Rein and Imperatrix.* Many people lived in it. On the last floor in my grandmother's house, the rooms had no windows. Instead of windows they had dormers through which the sun would come, and when it rained the raindrops would beat steadily and rhythmically on the thick opaque glass. So high, the place was quiet and peaceful like an oasis in the turmoil of the city. Like a windmill with a silent moving of its sails. In circles, perpetual and silent, with a invisible yet omnipresent wind.

My windmill.

I retreat into it periodically onto the mountain on which the mill sits, splendid and remote.

I climb its stairs, that are winding up high, just like the stairs in the big old house in which the rain beats the dormers, and the sun tries to sneak in. In the room on top, the floor creaks as I step in, complaining about being disturbed.

I sit on the wooden chair that my grandfather made in front of the plain little table with four wooden legs. On the table are my books and a bouquet of flowers that my grandmother would put there in season and also when I would return to her.

The stone walls of the mill are built to last. The windows are narrow slits through which one may look to the green hills beyond.

At times it appears like an old medieval castle in which resides a captive queen, imprisoned there for life, with the impossibility of escape. I look though the window slits into the distance and listen to the silent moving of the windmill's sails. It is a moment of solitude. But when I become too lonesome, my grandmother visits and talks to me. She may talk to me about past times. She is kind and does not reprimand me because I have left her alone on the last floor of the big house.

She is kind.

She brings me flowers to put on the table with four wooden legs where I sit and send my notes and missives to a nowhere world in a nowhere city. But the missives are real, as real as life.

The old palazzo has become a modern building. Its walls are being refurbished, the interiors divided into elegant condominiums. And instead of the windmill sails, an elevator goes up and down silently and without noise.

All is well. I am peaceful while the elevator runs up and down, and the sails of the mill move in silent circles.

Going Home

The wings of the mill are moving silently while I gaze through the narrowness of the window into the outer world.

There is a green vastness in front of me, and beyond the trees there is a body of water. I cannot see the water. Is it the River running peacefully through the fields of corn and soy beans with the vineyards behind it. The vine trees are in orderly rows; are their branches spread large and symmetrical as so many Menorah in a great temple of mother nature? Is this the same peaceful River that becomes a dangerous threatening torrent in the time of heavy rains or is it a sea with its changing colors and its changing moods?

I am going home.

My grandfather is taking my hand and we are strolling hand in hand on the marina where the big ships come and go. He buys me an ice-cream cone and I watch the ships. Big black ships that carry cargos.

I am awed by the ships, but he tells me that it is nothing. The times of the real, big ships that he was on in his younger days are gone. Gone, it seems, forever.

He is not bitter.

Times do change.

It is good to remember.

Grandfather is so tall and he takes long strides, and I try very hard to keep up with him with my ice cream cone. His work is now sporadic, but he always brings me a gift when he comes home from the sea. He calls me "bella mia" and strokes my hair with his large, strong hand.

In the afternoons I walk with my grandmother from San Nicolò, the nearby small Piazza, and from there to the large Piazza Grande, that looks out to the sea. The grand piazza is surrounded by very large neoclassical palaces, and in the middle stands a very decorative fountain with many allegorical sculptures. There is also a tall clock tower, and an old lady that sells corn kernels to the children who feed the pigeons. In the café, elegant old gents in the early evenings before suppertime sit with their wives and sip coffee or an aperitif watching the sea and enjoying the breeze.

It is the city's drawing room.

There are always children in the piazza. Many children, and we ask each other:

"Would you like to play?"

We run sometimes, pushing a ball, or just run around together on the grand piazza.

My childhood.

After a long time, grown up, I am coming back again to walk on the jetties, and to inhale the smell of the sea. And the smell of the sea grass that grows on the bottom of the beaches, between stones covered with algae mixed with the perfumes of the exotic plants from the nearby park.

I listen to the cry of the sea gulls. I think of my old aunt who would take me to the outskirts of the city from where we would see the lighthouses, hear the seagulls and eat fish grilled with oil and parsley leaves.

She is not with us anymore but her daughter takes me around to see the city again. I try to look at it with her eyes. She takes me to see the palaces that have been restored and refurbished. I look at their neoclassical architecture and we discuss the different friezes, and pointed lintels. In her home, we again eat fish that is seasoned with those same ingredients. It was caught in the nearby lagoon and tastes the same as it did many years ago. My cousin lives in a building with high ceilings and tall windows that have a large sill to lean on to observe the busy street below.

We walk again through the familiar streets.

I reminisce.

She tells me: "Your grandparents' house has been totally modernized. The apartments are full of light, have hardwood floors and modern kitchens in the American style."

I remember my grandmother's kitchen with an old stove and a red brick floor on the last floor of the "palace." The stove had a hood with a valance around it that she had sewn and put there by herself. My cousin says: "Let us go in and see. You would like it. I was there and did like it very much. Your grandparents' place is all redone. Do you want to see?"

I was born there.

I shake my head. I do not want to see. I want to remember how it was long ago.

We leave each other, my cousin and I. I walk through the streets of the city all by myself. It is a city, not just any old town in the provinces. There is a crowd of people everywhere.

The cars. The buses.

I walk alone and look at the buildings. Some are dark with age, with unwashed windows, the paint peeling. They may house storage or deposits for different merchandise. Some are clean looking with sparkling windows hung with curtains and flowerpots on small terraces. Some entrances are so large that an automobile easily passes though, and there is a sign that the passage is "Carrabile." I walk and avoid San Nicolò. James Joyce lived there once but that was well before my time. Walking through the crowds I listen to different languages spoken. It is a cosmopolitan city. Elderly, well-dressed ladies talk to each other using a quaint and elegant local dialect. It is still used, and it is alive. My cousin speaks to me in a perfect literary language. I have been away for so long. She is sure I have forgotten.

I feel strange among all those people rushing through the streets, and yet I feel at home. My mother had carried me in her womb through those streets. Perhaps I do remember.

This is my life.

I watch it through the windows of the windmill and the Adriatic is there with a smell of salt, mixed with the aroma of pine trees and the exotic plants brought there and planted by a Hapsburg prince.

The River runs lazily through the fields of maize, soybeans and some vegetable plants.
The River feels tired. It has seen so many changes. Too many tragedies and too many heroisms. It lazily runs into the sea in silence.
It is peaceful. It is good to remember.
When Sister calls and tells me to join her for dinner, I say that I will come.
And then,
I pick up my scarf and leave.

Trieste 2002

The Death of the Pine Tree

On a Sunday morning, she drives herself from the church back to her home. She rides on the avenue that is flanked by tall trees. She always greets the trees, tall and green. She does not know their names or species.

The avenue runs parallel to a park. It is a big park, full of flowers that grow under the trees: white, red, purple. There are bicycle routes for children to ride on. Mothers sit on the folding chairs watching children and dogs playing. Some of the mothers are leafing through magazines. No books. One cannot concentrate in the park watching children.

She thinks how good it is to be able to enjoy a cool summer day, sitting or walking through the park full of trees, flowers and children on bicycles and the dogs running after them.

But she herself never does that. She is not able to. Always a drive to go somewhere, to do something urgent to reach out to some unknown chimera.

She speeds up quickly, passing the park. On this balmy summer day, after the heat has finally receded, she stops to see Sister on her way.

Looking through the window of Sister's home onto the group of trees that have survived the onslaught of builders, she thinks that the trees keep each other company, like a semi-abandoned village that is trying hard to survive.

She watches the green village and sees that the pine tree she has often admired is not there any more.

"The pine tree?" she asks her Sister and the Sister responds: "It was growing too tall, too opulent. Other trees were squashed by the pine. There was no room for them to grow. It was necessary to cut down the pine."

Tall, majestic, throwing a dark shadow with branches that smelled of Christmas.

One, sacrificed for many. For the smaller, less perfumed, less vital?

She watches the spot were the pine stood healthy and beautiful. And now, there is emptiness.

The death of the pine tree.

"I miss you, friend," she thinks and says nothing. No more Christmases in fall and spring and in the summer heat. Such are the rules.

"But you had a splendid life my friend. You were cherished and admired." Requiescat in Pace.

After the dinner, she turns away from the window and sits in the chair in front of the television. With Sister she shares a glass of wine and they listen to the news together.

The cat sits in the corner on her pillow and watches over them. Her green eyes are just narrow slits in the whites of her orbits, in the head that is snow white just like the rest of her body. What does the cat think? The cat knows.

She watches the green slits of the cat's pupils and thinks: *It is time to return back home.*

My Magnolias

A long row of magnolia trees are swaying in the wind. The wind, from the sea and the mountains, comes walking through this island full of sun. The sun disappears occasionally behind the clouds that will bring rain, sheets of rain.

Gusts of wind shake the magnolia trees, a whole row as if a symphony has started and keeps continuing. I watch these trees with their rich mane of foliage, and the white flowers in the middle of the green leaves that glitter in the summer air.

One white flower sits in the middle of the tree unperturbed like a chalice that should not be touched by human hands. It does not sway. It does not move. I ask myself why the wind does not shake this white chalice, exposed to the rain and the capriciousness of the weather?

Another white flower is leaning toward my balcony, toward me. Its petals are opening, spreading, reaching out as if asking for help.

Two flowers for me, for my rainy days. One majestic in its silence and its arrogance. The other reaching to me, asking for help. White, untainted, unbruised, reaching out, spreading the immaculate petals, asking for help.

My flowers.

I will leave both, as we humans do, cruelly, unfeeling. Forgetting and getting on.

My magnolias.

The rain falls in sheets, the wind blows and shakes the trees. When the sun comes, will the flowers give up and die? But then, others will come next spring, and the spring after. The magnolias

will continue with their cycles of life.
Where will I be?

Grado 2002

Deceptions

There are two ways I would want to die.

I would die on a bench, in summer, on the Lago Di Garda, looking out onto the water. Just die. I have this vision of myself on the lake and whenever I get tired and forgetful, I imagine myself sitting on the bench and slowly disappearing. The bench, my secret amulet, my secret good luck charm.

I will run away from the nursing home, from hospitals with smelly rooms in which one pretends to be living. Instead, I will pack a small suitcase, buy an airline ticket and leave. Then I will get into a small pensione on the Lago and each morning I will walk to the bench and wait. My eyesight would be weak and in spite of the sun I will feel chilled. But that would be okay.

In the afternoon I will buy a small piece of Capodimonte with flowers. A bucket filled with flowers. Modern. Not very valuable. But it would remind me of another piece, more precious, that I had left at home. I love my home. But I want to die traveling to the Lakes.

When I was young, I had many admirers. My family was wealthy and I was spoiled. We traveled, I flirted. We moved and I got married. It was different to live in the States, but I was the same person. I still loved the same things. Still traveled, enjoyed good food and a glass of white wine, watching the flowers, the waters flowing, and the smell of pine trees.

When I take my last trip I want to do the same: listen to the water, watch the horizon above, smell the pines. And hopefully, when it gets very chilly for me at midday, when the sun is beating the earth, I will die.

81

I know it is a very poetic thought and wish. But it makes me feel so good. At times, though, I think that my romantic wish is very unrealistic. This happens when I wake up in the morning and my bones ache and my head is heavy on my neck and I can hardly get out of bed. It is then I think that traveling to my beloved bench would be quite impossible. So I get out of bed and take a hot shower and try to do some stretching exercises. And I think the day will come when my friends will not wish to see me anymore or will start feeling sorry for me. I, then, will decide not to see them. Never again.

This, then, is my other way to die. I will lock myself in my house and stop eating or will eat very little. Every day eating a little less. I will lose weight and become very thin. Then slowly I will stop taking fluids. This is going to be more difficult and will take more time. Slowly, I will become dehydrated and the lady that does my shopping and my cleaning will not notice how bad I look. She will think that I am getting just very old. One morning, she will come in with her packages, her vacuums and her detergents, and will find that I am gone.

Wonderful possibilities.

Since I have no children and only a few good friends, no one will be terribly sad. There would be some talk when old ladies get together for lunch or the coffee and cake, and perhaps they will be frightened for some time. This also shall pass.

Wonderful possibilities.

But at present, I will not dwell on it. It is a noontime and my serotonin seems adequate.

So I will have my tea, and for lunch I will have a salad of lettuce and tomato and a half-glass of white wine. In the afternoon, I will wait for the telephone to ring and someone to talk to.

Part III:
Walking Through the Mists

There are Many Homes

How many years have passed since she had seen this parched land, burned by sun, covered with boulders and sparse little bushes of survivors plants? A land where nothing grows for long, and after a while dies because of drought, poor terrain and neglect.

Out of her distant past, she remembers the olive trees with their abundant fruits. The fruits would be squeezed into the virgin olive oil with old-fashioned large, round stones that grounded the olives. The stones being moved around in circles by a pair of oxen. Was this in another century, in another time, when she was a daughter of the "Lord of the Manor," a staid little mansion filled with pretense and make believe?

Now, no more olive trees with their silvery leaves and the green fruits that slowly would become dark and succulent.

No more olive trees.

They burned out in a succession of fires that destroyed them and left bare the ground with stones, flecks of red dirt and no vegetation at all. What used to be beautiful olive groves became a bare back of the hills, devoid of trees, devoid of plants, ugly and repugnant.

"Where are the groves?"

"Why don't you plant them again?"

"What happened?"

She asks and they shrug their shoulders: "arson probably" they say without emotion.

There are still some vine trees left and they sell wine to buy the mere necessities. They also doctor the wine, add sugar to it to make it thicker and darker and they feel as if they will be able to deceive somebody.

"No one is going to buy your doctored wine," she tells them, but they do not listen. They do not care.

The young ones have left the land because they could not live off it. They just ran away.

A few are left, tied to the land, roaming the hills, cutting the dead tree branches to burn in fireplaces. In the back of the houses they plant broccoli, string beans, tomatoes. In the corner, there is a fig tree that produces especially large fruits that everybody admires. This is in the corner of the "Lord of the Mansion" garden. Others have small, shrunken trees with small, shrunken fruits that they dry in the sun and save for the winter.

In all this, there is a kind of beauty only the land can offer, not the cities, and felt more in the souls of the people than what the eye is able to see.

In the winter, water runs down the denuded hill in front of the enclosed garden and freezes, forming long hanging chandeliers of frozen ice. Children love to look at it, would like to touch it, but are forbidden. They stay in the garden with the fig tree in the corner of it and look longingly into the outside world.

Is there an escape to all this?

"Why didn't you escape, little brother?"

"Because you did not take me with you." his answer is in her head, since he does not speak any more.

"You would not have come," she said and knows his answer.

"This is my land, big sister. I am a soldier and I fight for it."

The soldiers have come home, back to the parched land, to the homestead. Some do not come. Some are sick but do not want help. They feel that they have lived long enough. What did they accomplish? It is hard to know.

He is back to the land he has always loved. Back to the half dilapidated "lord's manor," where the wind blows though the broken windows, and the roof is leaking when the rain falls. Laurel trees still grow between the boulders, wild and free. Their fragrant leaves are used in fish and vegetable dishes to add spice to the simple foods they prepare.

She never liked the taste of laurel. Give me "basilico," rosemary, sage.

The laurel trees grow wild.

In the garden, the lady of the house plants zinnias along the path that leads to the house. In summer, bees and butterflies crowd the flowers. Little streams of water run through. At their source, they are cool and drinkable.

"When are you coming to see me?" little brother asks. He is thin with a high blood pressure and poor appetite. He works lovingly in the garden. He has a family. A wife and children that help fix things up. In fall, they pick up grapes and figs and delight in them. Life is delightful.

"Next summer I will try," she answers and the summer passes by.

She is busy. She has so much and so much to do: jobs, trips, friends and her own family.

Next summer.

In the next summer, there is nothing important on her agenda. She is free. She makes arrangements, buys airplane ticket, orders her suitcases. All is set.

"We have many flowers in the garden," he says. "I will drive you around. When you come, we will meet you at the airport, my daughters and I."

"Shall I recognize you?" she jokes and he answers:

"You will. They tell me that I look exactly like our grandfather." Tall and thin. He smokes. He drinks too much red wine. He eats very little.

She is all set and boards her airplane. When she arrives at the local airport after changing to a smaller plane, little brother is not there to wait for her. His daughters meet her at the airport. (She hates airports.) He could not wait any longer.

****

She is carrying a big bouquet of red carnations. They are standing in the little cemetery where all the local people are buried. The graves are marked by "fraternities:" carpenters, ironworkers, farmers. Where are the soldiers to be buried?

She is there with his wife and his two daughters. They brought her there. He had a stroke and went into a coma. A massive cerebral hemorrhage. He never came out of it.

"So, little brother, why didn't you wait for me?"

"Why didn't you come sooner?" she hears his voice in her head. "I waited long enough."

In the middle of this arid countryside where olive trees are burned out but laurel is still growing, your grave is here and you are talking to me. You have left the mountain. You always wanted to return home.

The mountain is sobbing. It is shaking and the stones are falling down to cover the dead warriors. The night is shrouding the mountain in blackness. Warrior's blood makes the red flowers grow.

Red mountain, red flowers, red blood, but the little cemetery has only stone heads and there is a large bouquet of red carnations on this new grave.

"I am glad you came," she hears his voice whispering in the leaves. "We are together again, for a while."

"Why did you have to die?" she asks angrily, but she knows what the answer is.

"You left and did not come back in time."

The family stands around, at a distance, as if to give her time to talk to him alone. They have cried, already, all their tears. They are quiet and somber.

She gets up from kneeling at the grave and embraces them all, feeling that they are one family. Feeling together, grieving. In her head she feels him smiling, and is pleased that they are hugging and loving each other in his presence.

They are also smiling, and the red carnations are throwing a red shadow on their paths.

Ghosts

She is sick.

She lives in a darkened room with a glass door leading onto a balcony. She does not open the windows or pulls up the shades. She does not exit to the balcony. She imagines that the outside world has disappeared, perhaps into another dimension into another time.

Science fiction or a mental disease?

Or just an intellectual melancholia.

Walking around not knowing what to do with her small meal getting cold on the kitchen table.

The world tries to intrude upon her thoughts and upon her misery with its reality of the seasons. The reality of wind, cold, rain. Snow. And with the background noise of the war games.

"This war is killing me," she thinks and then speaks aloud, waiting for an answer. In her dark room, the oxygen level is reduced to a minimum. She knows that she should open the shutters, the door leading to the balcony and let the air get in.

She knows that she should pick up her gear and go.

"Where to go?" she asks herself, feeling trapped.

The world is receding again, getting further and further away until it disappears into an unknown distance like two parallel lines that meet in the infinity. She hears the noise of cannons, the machine guns with their repetitious piercing sound and thinks that her imagination is playing tricks on her memory. It just may be that there are no cannons or machine guns any more but precision bombs thrown from air machines, the super tanks, the fields full of land mines. The missiles and the rockets.

Progress.

"Why are you torturing yourself?" he speaks to her inside her head. "The wars have been part of the human race from the beginning. Remember the ancients. Remember the moderns. Remember. Remember. It goes off and on forever. It is with us as the seasons are, as the floods, the storms and the hurricanes."

"You want me to accept it. Is it why you are telling me this?" she asks without speaking loud.

" I want you to open the shutters and to go outside into the world. You are alive and are in need of a 'wander out' and a 'remember.' The second page is always the first."

She listens again in her head and hears a marching rhythm of the songs that the soldiers have sung through the times. The songs are invigorating, full of strength, which the togetherness and camaraderie conveys to the people. She sees him marching, carrying his heavy gear, singing and being happy.

"Were you there," she asks with some irony, "to fight the Assyrians and the Mesopotamians? The Sumerians? Or were you with them when they were destroyed and absorbed with nothing left but some obscure letters written in stone that occasionally were uncovered and possibly decoded?"

She knows that this is a theoretical question. But cannot stop asking.

"Were you with Jan Sobjeski at the door of Vienna. Do you remember the Ostrogots and the Visigoths? The Slavs and the Mongols?"

"No," he silently answers and she thinks that he is amused. "Those were not my fights. I have marched with my own hymns."

In her head she listens to him talking:

"We build and we destroy. We rise from the dust of the past and sometimes get destroyed in turn. It is the waves of time, happenings that sometimes we cannot grasp. The past, the present and the future merge into one gray and confusing mess. Only pieces are dug out. We try to remember and we try to understand."

"What remains?"

"I do not know," he answers to her. "Something does. For different people, different things remain. Music. Sunsets. The human thriving for betterment."

"And the marches?" she asks, "and the cruelties?"

He smiles and she feels his smile reaching out to her.

"Open the window and let fresh air in."

****

She peers through the window and sees the fog getting thicker. The bare tree branches are pointing toward the sky, naked, anemic, hostile. Was Jesus nailed on one of those trees?

The trees are scary.

She stops looking, and in the semidarkness of the room she feels alone as if the world does not exist. The world does not care. It is reckless, alien and not loving.

"Think how good it was when we were children," he comes again and tells her, "there are good times to remember. We used to fight with each other and run through the garden."

"Yes," she answers and adds cynically, "The Garden of Eden."

He leaves her thoughts and she is alone again. He does not like that she is so bitter. Knowing that, she tries to relax.

"Perk up girl," she tells herself, trying to be funny. "This too shall pass," she tells herself, walking through the rooms collecting the half-read newspapers.

****

Waking up early in the morning, she feels tired and discouraged. Passive. This is the time of the day when she would like to be dead.

Depression.

Is her blood glucose making her so, or does the morning awakening lack the adrenaline rush? That could be an easy interpretation by a scientific medic, or a poorly understood all embracing diagnosis of "a morning depression" treated with some modern pharmacological miracle. But she feels differently.

Pressure.

"This war will finish me," she says to him, speaking in her head.

"Looking back, would you have changed anything?"

"Why change? We all live our lives the way we see fit and at the end all is the same."

"The same? Nothing is the same. Ever. The change is the same."

"Death is the same," he says in her head. "That never changes."

The morning is easing into midday and into the afternoon. She collects her energy and peeks again through the window.

Mist, fog, haze.

Oxygen diminishes to a dangerous level and she finally opens the shutters and lets the fresh air in.

There is silence and she waits for him to speak again.

A Girl Named Sierra

I.

They were all waiting there to die. It was not a pleasant death. Their time had not come naturally, and most of them were quite young.

Men stood around grinning, savoring the women's fear and preparing themselves for the orgy of the massacre. Some were wearing guns, some long pointed knives.

"There are so many different kinds of guns!" she thought to herself. " I was never able to remember how many."

The women were afraid. Some were crying loudly while others were only trembling and making small, pitiful noises.

The men's bodies were sweaty and bloated. Their faces were beefy and dense.

They have no soul, she thought. *They are devoid of soul.* While standing in the front row of the mass of women, she felt as if her body and mind were distancing themselves from all of them.

The air was shimmering in layers of light as if the midday sun was hitting ocean waves. She stood up and bent forward into the timeless shivering of air as if from a great distance away. She was watching the men advancing in slow motion. Their closeness was emanating a repugnant odor of rotten flesh.

Then, all at once, she raised her arms above her head and looked upon the sky, calling loudly, "O Kali, my fierce mother and queen, whose arms reach far to punish thine enemies, and Demeter whose rage made the Gods tremble. To all my mothers, like Persephone, we have been raped again. You, my mother Kali, give me your strength and power that I may destroy these soulless creatures!"

She felt her body lose its weight, and felt herself growing larger, protecting the rest of the women with her body. The women stood behind her, moving in waves, and she knew then that the assassins would kill them but they would not be afraid.

She looked at the man who was approaching her with a knife. She fixed her eyes upon him, stretching her hands, spreading her fingers and invoking the Goddesses. She told him sternly, nauseated by the odor of his sweat. "Soul," she said, "You have no soul." She felt the knife plunge into her neck. The man slashed her throat. Blood ran down her body, wetting her breasts and staining the ground on which she was standing. The girl named Sierra was dead.

All the women were killed that same day and thrown into a common grave.

II.

In the beginning, it was only a rumor: a strange woman was seen in the countryside and no one knew where she came from.

Someone said a man was found dead—"one of them"—possibly of a stroke or a heart attack. There were other stories but nobody knew exactly whether there was any truth to them. And then, more things started to happen....

"A woman is walking through the countryside. Sometimes she is tall and thin with a mane of yellow hair tangled in knots. Sometimes she has dark skin, jet-black hair and sometimes she looks like someone who has not eaten for days. She breathes fire, cries over the dead and consoles the living. And sometimes she kills."

III.

The name was "Sonia's Bar." But it was only a bordello where women of different ethnicities were forced to prostitute themselves.

At the bar, "they" drank their aquavite, told their gruesome stories, sweated, laughed, and then raped the women.

Women were nothing. Men took care of their guns, their jeeps and their Ferrari's, and the women were less than nothing. Belonging to different races and different ethnic groups, the men never thought of comparing the women to their own mothers and sisters. They actually did not think of them at all. Women were only objects, spoils of war.

One evening, an old woman walked up to Sonia's Bar. The weather was changing from fall into winter, and the cold air outdoors was clear and invigorating. It was threatening to snow, to be the first snow of the season, but instead of the snow, rain suddenly started falling in sheets as if the heavens had opened up all at once.

The men ran indoors, leaving their heavy gears and their jeeps in front, crowding into the bar and warming themselves up with alcohol.

As she came in, she looked old, small and gray. In nondescript clothes, her face was wrinkled with tufts of gray hair sticking out from under the kerchief that was tied under her chin. Her clothes were drenched with rain, and her lips were purple. She looked as if she were freezing. No one paid any attention to her.

A young woman stirred in the corner with a drink in her hand. The old one sat next to her and touched her arm. Her hand was dry, fingers strong and pointed.

"How many of you are here?" the old one asked.

"I don't know," answered the young woman. "We don't count, and we don't talk to each other. We are ashamed of ourselves. Have a drink. This is the only way to survive." She looked up from her drink and saw the elderly woman, gray and nondescript with a kerchief on her head with tufts of gray hair sticking out from under the kerchief.

"What are you doing here?" the young woman exclaimed all at once, suddenly alarmed. "Get away from here! These animals may even force you—"

"Into prostitution?" The old woman finished her sentence.

"Where is your home?" she continued, speaking in a monotone and without raising her voice.

"I have no home—my village was destroyed and we were brought here. And after this, I could not go home anyway." Her lower lip began to quiver but she kept back her tears. "It is finished for us."

"Get away from here," the young woman repeated harshly, and moved to the other side of the room.

The old one followed after her and then turned her back to her as if to protect her.

"Who is this?" A man had noticed the elderly woman and started walking toward her. "What is your business here?"

"I came to see the women," the old woman answered patiently, looking him in the eye.

"Where do you come from?" he asked.

"I come from the dead," she answered peacefully. "You killed me some time ago. I am buried not too far from here."

Others were approaching and made a semicircle around her.

"A woman's body belongs to her only. Not to you and your war games. She may do with it whatever she wishes. You'd better let the women go."

"Whoever you are, you will be dead tonight, you old mummy," the man said.

Her body became straight now, very straight, and her arms lifted. She appeared taller as the crowd kept approaching, and her arms moved faster and faster until flames seemed to spurt from her fingertips. Soon the whole room was full of flames and the screams of people mixed with the smell of burning flesh. The old woman pulled the frightened girl out of the burning inferno. Her face was different now, not old anymore but dark and foreboding and of an immense, cruel beauty.

"Who are you?" the frightened girl asked while running away from the burning building.

"I am Sierra. I was killed not too far from your village and buried in a common grave with so many other women. I am all those women. But today I am primarily Kali, the goddess of rage, the cruel goddess who does not forgive, and who punishes those who cross her. Go home and take care of your people. There are still some of them left—women, children and young boys. When all of this is over, bring flowers and incense to our graves."

She became small and gray again—and walked into the night.

The rain had long since stopped, and the smell of oncoming snow was again in the air, mixed with the smell of burning. Sonia's Bar was no more.

IV.

They had killed her son at sunset, with many others. She was able to take his body and bring it next to the chapel that stood at the margin of the road.

The road led through the trees and its borders were studded with small, votive chapels that people had built through time as thanks for received graces.

It was night and she had thrown a blanket over his body as if to protect him from the night cold. She was rocking back and forth as a small child might do. The tears had dried out and she hoped that she herself would die that same night.

A woman came and sat next to her. She was dressed in black, her head covered, her face sallow and dark as if parched by the sun.

"I came to help you," she said, embracing her. "I came to help you mourn and to bury your son." She sat near her. She sat near her for a while without a word. Then she stood up and told the mother, "We are going to bury him at the foot of the chapel. And when this madness is over, the green grass will grow on his grave. You will bring flowers and there will be flowers for all the others that don't have a grave and were not buried here."

She picked up the body, wrapped in his mother's blanket, as if she were picking up a loved child and deposited him in the grave. She broke a few branches of a nearby evergreen and gave it to the mother.

"Instead of flowers," she said.

The mother threw the branches into the grave on top of her son's body. She murmured prayers for the dead as her people had done throughout the centuries; then they threw soft dirt mixed with stones into the grave and made it so that it appeared no different from the rest of the hill.

"His monument will be the chapel," the woman said, "the chapel was put here to fulfill a promise." She embraced the mother and stroked her hair and then told her, "Go back to your village and console the others."

"There is nothing left for me," the mother said.

There are other women who have lost, and there are children as well as grown ups who need strength. After these words, the mother felt stronger and more peaceful.

I will go, and in the spring we will bring flowers and pray on his grave for all our dead children."

"Where do you come from?" she asked the woman whom she did not recognize. "You don't live in these parts."

"I am also a mother. At times I am angry and I punish and destroy. But today I am mostly a mother whose son has been taken away from me and whom I have buried in a borrowed grave. There will be no spring this year and there will be no autumn. Springs and autumns will be very scarce. Demeter will not give us any. People that travel between villages with guns and knives will be dying with frost and cold. But you try to survive with each other and take care of the children."

"Your son was also killed?" asked the mother.

"Yes," was the reply. "He was crucified. That happened a thousand years ago."

She embraced the mother, then spread her arms as if blessing her, and then waved good-bye, her face radiant, bathed in the moonshine.

"Stay well, my daughter," she said and walked into the forest.

The mother walked down the path and into the ruined village.

V.

"They" were attacking the village from all the hills and mountains that were above the valley. Nothing much left now except a few houses that still stood where women and children hid in hunger and fear. The winter was brutal and little food was left for them. But the murderers persisted in their business of assassination. They must have known that only women and children were left in the ruins that once was a village.

There was no spring or fall that year. Nothing grew on the countryside. Adolescent girls ventured into what was left of the vegetable gardens and dug the roots of herbs and the roots of long-dead dandelion plants. They brought them home to their mothers to cook. The boys stayed close to their mothers and did not venture outdoors. The children wrapped themselves in worn out clothes and old newspapers in order to resist the cold.

The shelling continued through the heart of the winter and always the possibility of "them" descending into the villages was very real. Villagers had heard of the strange woman and were hoping that she would come. She would come at the strangest times, but many people still did not believe she existed.

Then one night, when it was particularly cold and the moon was very clear, the villagers heard strange noises emanating from the hills above. It was a mixture of human screams and animal howls that filled them with terror and fear

It lasted all night long and in the morning when they dared to come out of their hiding places. They saw whole packs of wolves leaving the countryside. A silence had fallen over the valley, and when the bravest dared to go out to investigate, they found her seated on a large rock beside the snow-covered road outside the village. A gray wolf was seated patiently at her feet. She looked lean and undernourished. Her face was gray and drawn, her lips pursed and protruding. She looked a lot like the gray wolf sitting next to her.

"The men in the bunkers above the valley are all dead," she told them. "The wolves were hungry and attacked them. The winters are brutal and the wolves are desperate. There are no sheep or any other animals to attack. Not even dogs exist. When spring comes, bury the soldiers in a common grave and build a great heap of stones upon them as your ancestors did in ancient times. The boys should throw the soldiers' arms away and not try to use them. By the time spring comes, the arms will be all rusted from the ice and snow. The wolves are also all gone; there will be no more wolves. Save the water from the thawing snow and try to plant the greens again when the spring comes."

She got up from her seat and looked over the small crowd of women and children. She raised her hands slowly as if to offer a benediction, and then dropped them again. The gray wolf next to her, slowly raised his body and stretched. The woman turned around and walked away, followed by the wolf. Their traces in the snow would soon disappear.

VI.

Sierra walked along through the towns and villages. She walked through streets with broken-down homes, burned barns, and destroyed houses of worship.

Remembering how it once was, she roamed the countryside as herself—a woman who was killed and then thrown into a common grave. Trees were chopped down or burned, the red-tiled roofs smashed. The grass was replaced by mud and slime.

She walked and remembered when the countryside was green with trees in the hills and birds nesting and singing in the trees. The valley was green. The villages were full of life with their rituals of spring and autumn, and girls and boys meeting each other at sunset.

Her mother had read books about forests in faraway countries and fell in love with dense woods, waterfalls and exotic birds. When her daughter was born, she named her Sierra. Sierra carried the name as a symbol, as a promise and a memorial to a mother who fell in love with strange and distant countrysides.

Sierra remembered her first dates and her first love. A boy that was a poet and dreamer. They would sit on the stone benches on the side of the narrow roads that led through the hills and look down at the valley, imagining sometimes to see the distant sea shimmering under the sun.

She left him in order to go far away and they wrote letters to each other, full of melancholy yearning and desire for each other. The letters became less frequent and only memories remained.

She still remembered, it was good to do so. She was away a long time but always waiting to return, cherishing the memories without remorse or resentment and not being sorry. Always planning to return to the daintiness of the villages, to the squares full of people at sunset, to the bells announcing it was time to go home. The flowers in the fields and in the pots on the small terraces full of herbs with perfumed leaves that were put between bed sheets and women's garments.

She roamed the devastated countryside. She thought about men that perhaps she brought in from another life, or that perhaps was only a projection of her own imagination.

She was a painter, a sculptor, a Pygmalion. She was a woman that carried her mother's dreams of strange and exuberant countries that existed somewhere far away.

And when she came back Sierra was killed with the others and thrown in a common grave. The exotic passage had disappeared forever. Now she roamed the devastated country alone with no bells or red-tiled roofs.

In some of the villages, mothers were still collecting children and keeping them together in cold little rooms. The boys stayed close to them, the girls venturing in the back of the houses digging roots in old vegetable gardens. Occasionally some of the boys would venture out for a short moment, too curious to stay indoors.

It was peaceful now—the soldiers were gone. The grass was starting to grow between the stones, and an occasional low bush of thorns was showing some green leaves here and there.

"Demeter, my mother, you are giving us back the spring," she whispered.

The dandelions will start to grow again if there are still roots left in the ground, and mothers may plant a few potatoes. Bushes with thorns will grow again first, then the flowers will come. Slowly other things will start to happen. People that left will return and start building. Children will play, laugh, cry and life will go on.

VIII.

She climbed the hill, light as the shadow that she was. The little scraggly bushes full of thorns were starting to grow and cover the countryside. Some small animals were running through the underbrush, making swishing noises.

She walked to the summit—an old abandoned monastery with a semi-destroyed temple, which was still perched on the top. Bushes and thorns were making an impenetrable barrier around it. She walked through the bushes and thorns. Her flesh could not be harmed. A serpent was sliding through the underbrush when she reached the top, and she put her foot on its head. The serpent stopped. When she removed her foot, it was not moving anymore.

She proceeded toward the temple. She entered the sanctuary through the opened door—the interior semi-dark and cold, long abandoned by humans, but still a holy place.

"Infinity," she said, "my brother Infinity."

"So you are coming back, Sierra," the voice said from the darkness.

"My brother Infinity," she lowered her head slightly, her dark cape covering her whole body and part of her face. "There will be no more torture of women. No more rape, murder, abductions and killing. Everyone will have a soul from now on. The soulless ones are destroyed."

"What about the men, Sierra?" Infinity asked.

There will be no more torture of women," Sierra repeated stubbornly. "No more killing, abduction or rape." In the sanctuary, her voice was like a prayer, like an Archangel's promise to humanity.

"Sierra, I was also tortured by the Romans. I was killed by them so many centuries ago."

"I remember that, my brother Infinity, since I was there with you. I stood there with you and many others, and shared the pain. I also helped lower you into a borrowed grave. I have many names: I am Ruth and Sarah and Mary, but I am also Judith who cut Holoferno's head to save her people. My mother is Kali and Demeter and the other goddesses. At different times I am one or all of them. I am also Sierra, who was killed not long ago and then thrown in a common grave. This will be again a holy ground as many others will be, and there will be flowers on our graves. It is time for me to be leaving."

"Farewell, Sierra, my sister," Infinity said.

"Farewell, Infinity, my brother, my son."

IX.

It is quiet around the countryside—the guns have been silent for some time. Children are walking cautiously from their places of hiding to the side of the road. They see her coming down the hill. The children know her and come, wishing to see her and to greet her. She comes close, her robe floating and her face covered with the cape. When she is close enough, her robe opens for the children to see that there is not a body between the dark folds, only a glow as if the light of the setting sun was filtering through. She stops for a moment as if to greet the children, then proceeds into the distance, getting smaller and smaller, and finally completely disappearing into the horizon. The children run home to tell the grownups that the lady in gray has gone away.

Goodbye to the Old House

The old house was creaking, whispering in the night with footsteps treading on the upper floor that Maggie knew were not real. The house itself was breathing heavy and sighing—perhaps complaining? Maggie thought so. She was the only one left in the house. It felt lonesome. No children running up and down the stairs with dogs following, cries and fights, and Sis yelling at them, "When are you going to stop your ruckus?"

They were all gone. The children were all grown up, married and now lived elsewhere. Sis found a place for herself closer to her workplace. Maggie buried her mother and father. She buried her English Setter and her Golden Retriever.

The house was all hers. With the seasons changing, her moods were affected. Winters became long with a touch of depression. The snow accumulating on the lawn, and ice on the driveway. They were precarious winters full of gray nostalgia.

Spring and summer came, the tulips and daffodils showing their colorful crowns. She put geraniums on the patio and seeds in the bird feeder. It was very peaceful with the birds just chirping. Some birds were similar to the swallows that she remembered from the old country. Then there were the others: robins, plump and colorful, red cardinals, some blue jays and a whole slew of little brown sparrows and finches, lively and aggressive, dancing on the patio. It was nice to sit and read a book, or meditate in solitude on the patio surrounded by evergreens.

The fall found her driving through rows of trees on the large suburban streets and the highways of New Jersey. The leaves changing their colors from brilliant yellow to translucent orange to magenta red to blood-red and then to a golden brown: maples, oaks, Japanese maples. Those were the magic colors of fall. The most beautiful time of the year.

Then the winter came and she would again be listening to the complaints and whispers of the old house. The snow fell and accumulated and the ice and the danger of slipping would be there.

It was in one of those winters with repeated snowstorms that piled inches upon inches of snow on the ground, that Maggie decided to sell the old house. Each winter, with its snow plowing and the dirty sidewalks, she would think about moving. Then when the season changed, she would give it another chance. But this time, this decision was final.

She thought, *Everything passes. Everything is due to change. Change is growth; change gives us the gift of memories. Memories are ours. Some of them buried deep in the subconscious and surfacing only in dreams, other staying vivid with us, talking to us, making us know that having memories means being alive.*

The house will survive, Maggie thought. *"Someone young and aggressive with an entrepreneurial spirit and a lot of money will remodel and reinvent the house. The house will become another house. It will lose its memories and its physiognomy. It will die to be resuscitated as someone else, like a phoenix out of ashes.*

But after she started emptying the drawers, looking through the closets and storage chests in order to prepare to move, it began to feel as if her past had been destroyed. It was as if she was cleansing herself and purifying herself of old, dusty objects. All things passed. Nothing seemed relevant—like giving away old clothes, like a serpent that changes her skin to build a new one.

****

She had to go to the basement to look through old file cabinets and storage bins. She hated basements. They reminded her of old, scary movies where horrible events always took place. Monsters and crazy men waiting to attack. But there were no bad spirits and werewolves in this basement, only storage bins, cobwebs and a cabinet with rusty hinges and creaky doors.

In one drawer she found a big, yellow envelope that had a name on it. Whose name was it? It was written in her own handwriting that had changed over the years but was still recognizable. It took some time, but memories returned. His name was Peter. The face came into focus, sharply and all at once: a long nose, hazel eyes, lips with an eternal cigarette he was sucking on as if it were mother's milk. Her first love: Peter. The letters that he wrote after they were separated, the ocean between them. Letters that she read avidly in the beginning, when she was missing him terribly. Then, slowly, the urge to read them diminished and they lay forgotten in the yellow envelope.

How does one resuscitate their first love? She sat on an old chair in the basement, closed her eyes, and held the letters in her lap.

It was a time immediately after the war, when parts of Europe were suffering with a lack of everything. Life was scarce of pleasantries.

They were both art students at the same university. Books were the only objects to which they had easy access. Externally, not many distractions were available. They spent most of their time together, in classrooms, libraries, walking through the mud on the periphery of town looking for some kind of food offered by farmers or black marketers. It seemed as if they were perpetually hungry and chronically adjusted to it. It was almost impolite to talk about food or the fact that they were both harboring hunger. Pretend, pretend, was the war cry.

Taking long walks in the spring and summer, sitting in cold, unheated rooms in winter, and sipping tea. Not much alcohol in those days. She remembered vividly the tea kettle, two cups, a few biscuits and not much more. They had their youth and each other. Sometimes colleagues and friends would join them and a few more cups would be taken out. Innumerable discussions about the state of the world would ensue, talk about books read, and yes, the brutal cold of the winter. Thinking of it, it was as if she had never left and at the same time it was also so foreign to her, she who at present was sitting in her large basement, trying to pack her possessions—some very important, valid and precious; some trivial, obsolete, useless.

He would ask, at times, casually, as if it was an afterthought, "Shall we get married?" Always an optimist, he anticipated a rosy future.

"Once we finish college, all is going to be better," he'd say.

Her father was in the States, separated from them by the war and the family was anxious to be together again.

"I want to leave. I want to do things, go to museums and large libraries. I want to feel the pulse of the big cities."

"How about me?" he would ask. "My father is not in the U.S."

"I will send for you, Peter," she would always promise, believing it.

How difficult to remember: he was so kind, soft spoken, caring. But Maggie was restless and always wanted to fun. Running, running—sometimes in circles and when given a chance, running far away.

When she finally boarded the train to leave, they were all crying: friends, relatives, and people who were standing around on the train platform. She and Peter held each other and she kept repeating, "I will write. I will come back. I will send for you." But of course she did not.

The distances. They wrote to each other letters full of yearning; teary, sentimental letters that spoke of loneliness and desire full of hope to see each other again. And when it became obvious that they would not see each other soon, if ever, the letters became shorter and further apart. In the last letter he wrote to her, he offered a hypothetical question: "Is it more important to have each other and share a warm cup of tea, or roam the world in search of big museums and libraries in the vastness without intimacy?" In that same letter he announced his recent marriage.

He had survived. It took her a long time to get over it. But she also survived. They both were young and energy was plentiful.

Should she destroy the letters? Should she keep the memory? Maggie put the envelope in the file cabinet, not destroying it but not reading it either.

****

Sis came to visit as she often did and found Maggie in the basement shuffling through the papers in the old file.

"What are you looking for?" she asked curiously. "Why don't you burn these old papers?"

Sis had never married. She was one of those rare people that were too cerebral to need a marriage or dependencies. She read voraciously everything worth reading: fiction, politics, geography, economics. Sis had an executive position that spelled power. Sis was totally pleased with herself, and when Maggie would suggest that perhaps she should be teaching and offer her knowledge to others, she would just smile and shrug it off. But she was honest, loyal and cared about Maggie and her children.

"I don't know Sis," Maggie answered. "Not yet. Let it sit here for a while."

"But that was such a long time ago," Sis said.

And she was right. Maggie has changed so. It was as if it happened to someone else. And yet, and yet....

"They are not old papers," Maggie thought. "They are mementos. They are me. The 'me' that I have long forgotten."

"Remember my first boyfriend?" she asked Sis.

"Vaguely," Sis said.

"I am not destroying these 'Maggie thoughts again.' But I am not going to read them either. I will put them away as old relics—old reminders. Perhaps some other time I may read or destroy them."

She then found another bunch of letters, neatly tied with a red ribbon, that her husband had written to her during their courtship. That was a period of her life when she was desperately trying to insert herself into an everyday lifestyle. To have a simple life, to settle down, to marry and to have children, cats and dogs and a big rambling house with lots of people in it.

Her husband had such a lifestyle. He was a good person. He did not have the qualities to be controversial or bad. Children came and she lived a life of convention, seeing friends, having house parties, driving children to school and activities. But except for her children, her parents, Sis and the dogs, it was a boring life. It felt sedentary and pedestrian with each day similar to the other. Did she have to do it? And was it worth it?

Years of sameness, years of days ensuing each other life soldiers in line: One, two, one, two. Her husband did not mind. He did not and could not understand. No adrenaline rush. No need for it. A book, a child's story, a music lesson. The conclusion was that it was okay. Nothing was lost. Nothing is ever lost as life is given to us to use it at different levels at different times.

When all the elders died and Sis moved away, their being together as husband and wife lost all value. When the children reached college age, they separated. There was no drama, only a bit of melancholy as at the funeral of an old friend who passed away. It was over quickly and she was running again.

****

Maggie is tearing and shredding old papers and it feels again as if she is purifying herself, downsizing, reducing life into a concentrated substance called importance, versus the ballast that has accumulated in her life over the years. Everyone's years. It is like taking a bath in very clear water, perhaps in a pristine waterfall as advertised on television. But the waterfall does not exist in our polluted world.

So few belongings to conserve and reduce to essentials. Sis grins and semi-tolerates purification.

"Do you have anything to throw away?" Maggie asks Sis, just to keep the conversation going. Sis makes her uncomfortable. Sis considers Maggie overly sentimental.

"No, I don't keep anything. If you are going to move, you should throw things away," Sis says. "They are superfluous. At this time, just useless papers accumulating dust."

Maggie continues. Most of the old papers are shredded and she feels lighter. Layers of old dried skin have been removed from her back. And yet, there are some papers she feels like saving. She finds another stack of letters, neatly conserved in a manila envelope together with an album. She remembers.

After running again after the divorce, she remembers the love affair that lived in the tropics. One of those fairy tales that is doomed from the beginning. She looks at the album and sees a picture of herself in a sundress, a flower in her hand, and next to her is he: Tall and handsome with the body of a strange, young god, elegant and slim.

He is a swimmer. He has large shoulders and a small waist. In the water, he is in his element like a young dolphin or a water spirit from some ancient Greco-Roman mythological tale.

She is not a water nymph. She is a woman in her forties, old by his account, a conventional city dweller. Is it worth it to live a fairy tale?

He takes her swimming, sailing, they live the water miracle. Water might have been their wedding bed. One long summer, then another, then yet another. And then she accuses him of not caring, she becomes too possessive, she wants to change him.

The summers are over. Maggie is holding the album and the letters he wrote. She peeks inside a few of the letters he has sent her, the feelings sweet and tender. Perhaps he did care.

She saves the letters and the album thinking that perhaps when her granddaughter grows up, with Maggie long gone, the young girl may find it interesting and exciting. It might have some tumulus to a young mind, wondering perhaps about a woman who had a taste for fairy tales and the temerity to do things differently.

Maggie has to rest, take some deep breaths, close her eyes and clear her mind. She does that, and the old house continues to sigh, creak and sing in whispers. She hears the soft treading of steps on the upper floors and knows that they are not real. It is the old house talking to itself.

"Where is the end?" Maggie asks herself out loud.

****

111

She looks through the window of her new home, across the space, and sees in the evening, when the air is clear, the light of New York City shimmering like a thousand little fires on the far horizon. Not Rome anymore, but New York is the Eternal City that she looks at from her New Jersey Hills. New York, where people live, love, pray, get angry and make peace with one another. Where the heart of the universe beats its strong, steady rhythm. She watches it emerge from the waters as if an enormous whale was lifting it up on its back to submerge it again and make it invisible when the fog engulfs all in the harsh winter time.

"It is a beauty," she tells herself, watching with fascination. Perhaps Merlin the Enchanter created it and makes it disappear in the mist, only to resurrect it again on a summer day.

****

Maggie walks her dog on a path in New Jersey. It is a September morning and the air is cool and invigorating. An early September day. It promises to be a clear and balmy day with no more summer heat accompanied by its heavy and oppressive humidity. It is 8:30 AM, and she savors the peace of the morning. The cars on the bottom of the hill swish by and it feels as if the ocean is near and is making the swishing noises. People rushing to work, cars passing, swish, swish, swish.

***

She enters her home, prepares herself for the day, has a cup of coffee. Her dog falls asleep on his pillow next to her chair. It's so peaceful. It's so idyllic.

And the horror is to begin.

The telephone rings and Sis is on the phone.

"Maggie, put on the television," Sis says. "They are bombing New York."

The trees, at this time of year, impede her view directly to the center of the universe that is Manhattan. She puts the television on and is horrified and speechless. The twin towers are crumbling as if they were props made of papier-mâché. Falling into dust.

Disintegrating. The heart of the city has been mortally wounded. The steel skeleton sticks out from the crumbling tower like the spine of a giant that has been broken in half and is ready to give up at any moment and fall into dust.

Dust to Dust.

The skyline is not there anymore. Clouds of smoke envelope what was once the floating fairy tale on the big River.

The crying of widows, the crying of mothers, the crying of innocents.

****

This is not a battle.

This is not a guerilla war.

This is the ultimate villainy, the ultimate ruthless villainous violence. And the ultimate of violence is a self-destruction.

The suicidal and cowardly villainy of it all!!

We are going to exorcize the demons and we are going to rebuild the Great City. The Great Heart is going to beat again, and the City is going to rise again out of the water on the back of the big whale. Merlin the Enchanter is going to walk with us on this most majestic site on the planet.

The old house and the memories all seem so distant: the ones that she destroyed and the ones that she carried with her. It all seemed unimportant, distant, minuscule. *It is time to look ahead,* she thinks to herself, *Time to bury the dead, to comfort the living, to remember, to build, and to say, 'Goodbye to the old house.'*

Maggie closes her eyes and prays silently for the City, the world and the universe.